Irina Prodan

The effect of weather on stock returns

A comparison between emerging and developed markets

Anchor Compact

Prodan, Irina: The effect of weather on stock returns: A comparison between emerging and developed markets. Hamburg, Diplomica Verlag GmbH 2013
Original title of the thesis: Is there a difference in the weather effect between developed and emerging markets: A comparison between markets around the world

ISBN: 978-3-95489-056-9
Print: Anchor Academic Publishing, an Imprint of Diplomica® Verlag GmbH, Hamburg, 2013
Additionally: Vrije Universiteit Amsterdam, Amsterdam, Niederlande, MA-Thesis / Master,

Bibliographical Information of the German National Library:
The German National Library lists this publication in the German National Bibliography. Detailed bibliographic data can be found at: http://dnb.d-nb.de

The digital publication (eBook) of this work with the ISBN 978-3-95489-556-4 can be purchased on the general market or directly from the publisher.

© Anchor Academic Publishing, ein Imprint der Diplomica® Verlag GmbH
http://www.diplom.de, Hamburg 2013
Printed in Germany

Abstract

One renowned and frequently researched anomaly over the last two decades is the weather effect – the impact of weather on stock market returns. The extensive literature on the weather effect fails to converge towards a unique, systematic and robust relationship between the weather and the stock market. Therefore, the aim of this paper is to explain the contradictory results in the literature by testing whether stock prices are affected by the weather in a significantly different manner depending on the level of market development and explaining how this difference behaves over time. In order to test for this, city-by-city, pooled and binary regressions are employed using data of 10 developed and 10 emerging countries over the period 1996-2011 by using two different means of seasonal adjustment. The results show that weather has a very small impact on the worldwide stock market returns and that the significance of the weather effect is decreasing over time with a cyclical pattern in terms of its recurrence. We identify the year 2001 as the cut-off point when the significance of weather on stock markets diminishes. No support has been found for a real difference in the weather effect between emerging and developed countries. However, evidence has been found of the relative inefficiency of the emerging markets and for the declining influence of weather in time.

JEL Classification: G10, G14, G15, O16

Keywords: Behavioral finance, weather effect, stock market returns, developed and emerging countries

Table of contents

1. Introduction

Advocates of the efficient market hypothesis argue that security markets are rational and that prices on these markets reflect the underlying economic fundamentals (Fama, 1970). Nevertheless, numerous market anomalies came to light over the past decades. A prominent complementary paradigm is that investors' trading behavior is shaped by psychological influences which are considered irrational. Shiller (2003) argues that this division of the financial literature - behavioral finance - is one of the most vital research areas.

One renowned and frequently researched anomaly over the last two decades, especially in the last years, is the weather effect. This can be defined as the effect that weather, measured using a variety of quantitative meteorological variables, has on the stock market returns. As argued by behavioral finance, economic agents have bounded rationality, allowing subjective factors to influence their decision making process. The weather effect is a pertaining component of this theory that can be placed within the psychology block of behavioral economics (Barberis and Thaler, 2003).

The extensive literature upon the weather effect has led to conflicting results. Starting with Saunders (1993), a considerable number of studies have found evidence supporting the impact that weather has on investors' mood and consequently on stock market activity. Further investigation and a variety of methodological approaches have revealed a lack of results consistency. The weather effect has been discovered to exist in many countries – United States, Taiwan, Thailand, Finland, but critics followed as well. Most opponent papers are in favor of a weak form of efficient market and claim that the existence of the weather effect is merely a result of inaccurate data definition, discontinuous records and data mining.

Given these prior contradictory results, our research study investigates whether emerging stock markets are prone to deviate from fundamentals and to display a persistent weather influence relative to developed and more efficient markets. In this paper, our aim is to test whether stock prices are affected by weather in a significantly different manner depending on the level of market development. A significant difference would then explain why financial literature on the weather effect is devoid of consensus.

We expect that the weather effect is more important in emerging countries relative to developed ones based on two arguments. First, emerging markets are more likely to be inefficient compared to developed countries (Harvey, 1994); therefore, stock markets are more exposed to anomalies that can be explained throughout means of behavioral finance. Secondly, the proportion of local investors to foreign investors is higher in developing countries (Korajczyk, 1996), which could mean that these markets are more influenced by a set of common factors and local conditions that affect local investors – such as weather.

We demonstrate, however, that there is no difference in the weather effect between developed and emerging countries. Also, we find evidence of a cyclical pattern of the weather effect. For both types of countries the weather effect is small (if existing) and the significance of the influence of weather is declining over time. Within the cyclical pattern of the weather effect, we identify a breakpoint for developed countries around the year 2001, followed by a breakpoint for emerging countries around the year 2002. Furthermore, although there is no difference in the significance of the weather effect in emerging and developed countries, we show that emerging countries are relatively less efficient than developed countries.

The remainder of this paper is organized as follows. Section 2 provides a review of the literature on the weather effect, followed by a description of the data collection process and data analysis in Section 3. The methodology and the results for the different tests are presented in Section 4. We check for robustness to seasonal adjustment method in Section 5. Finally, we provide some potential explanations of our findings in Section 6 and present the conclusions of this study in Section 7.

2. Literature review

The literature investigating the relationship between the weather and the stock market prices considers two distinct sections. First, psychology literature supports and explains the connection between weather and mood and the further link between mood and behavior. Second, financial literature can be used to explore previous research on the relationship between weather and the behavior of investors on stock markets while connecting it to stock market quantitative variables.

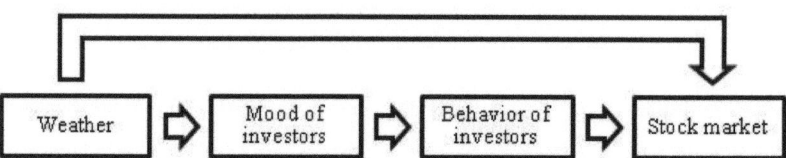

Figure 1: The relation between weather and the stock market (as used in financial literature)

Psychology literature - according to our knowledge – has not examined the direct link between weather and investors' behavior on the stock market. Therefore, we make use of the reasoning applied in all the previous financial literature on the weather effect: weather affects the mood of investors, the mood of investors influence investors' behavior and this reflects straightforward in stock market trading activity (figure 1).

2.1. Weather, mood and decision making behavior

Psychologists have studied the relationship between weather, mood and decision making behavior extensively. There are several links between weather (measured by different variables), mood (the relatively short state or quality of feeling at a particular time) and behavior.

Support has been found for the influence of environmental factors and weather conditions on the mood of individuals (Watson, 2000). Kals (1982) concluded that one third of the people are weather sensitive and that mood and health vary with changes in the weather conditions. The influence of various types of weather has been found to be significantly related to individuals' mood. Cunningham (1979) studied the relationship between weather (sunshine, temperature, humidity, wind and lunar phases), mood and behavior and found a significant result especially for sunshine and temperature. Howarth and Hoffman (1984) also noticed a positive effect of sunshine on mood when examining the effect of weather on mood variables. Their study concludes that sunshine leads to more optimism.

Further evidence has been found for the effect of humidity (e.g. Wyndham, 1969; Allen and Fischer, 1978; Howarth and Hoffman, 1984), wind (e.g. Denissen, Penke, Butalid and Van Aken, 2008), barometric pressure (Digon and Bock, 1966) and temperature (e.g. Bell and Baron, 1976; Howarth and Hoffman, 1984; Page, Hajat and Kovats, 2007) on mood. Anderson (2001) showed that low temperatures can lead to a more aggressive approach and high temperature to hostility or apathy. This in turn influences the risk taking behavior.

Loewenstein, Elke, Christopher and Welch (2001) argued that feelings and mood can affect behavior and decision making. When people are in a better mood they tend to have a more optimistic judgment about the future (Arkes, Herren and Isen, 1988; Bagozzi, Gopinath and Nyer, 1999). A good state of mind is related to overconfidence and less risk aversion. Therefore good mood can increase the likelihood of making riskier choices (e.g. Yuen and Lee, 2003; Kuhnen and Knutson, 2011), which can lead to poorer decision making (Au, Chan, Wang and Vertinsky, 2003). Johnson and Tversky (1983) observed that positive mood leads to optimistic choices whereas negative mood to pessimistic choices.

Another argument supporting our behavioral analysis is that the causes of the mood changes might have nothing to do with the choices being made (paramount when choosing a portfolio). In line with this argument, Schwarz and Clore (1983) concluded that mood influences decisions even when the cause of the mood deviation is not related to the decision that is to be made. This phenomenon is called 'mood misattribution' and it is an important component of behavioral finance. As a consequence, the mood variation (caused by different influences, for example the weather) has to be irrelevant for the efficient market hypothesis to hold because mood is not connected to the underlying fundamentals of assets.

In addition, Simon (1955) and Conlisk (1996) argue that investors face bounded rationality. They tend to choose satisfying decisions instead of optimal decisions. The feelings experienced when decisions are made by comparing the costs and benefits of different options deviate the decision in a different direction than is optimal (Loewenstein, 2000). Moreover, Forgas (1995) noticed that mood becomes more important for the risk assessment of the decision when the decision itself is more complex and uncertain.

Mehra and Sah (2002) directly related the effect of feelings and mood of investors on equity prices. As previously discussed, mood can affect the attitudes of people towards risk taking. The authors show that even small changes in mood can affect the prices of equities significantly if: the subjective parameters of investors (risk averseness, perceived discount rate) change over time by changes in the mood of the investors, a substantial part of the market participants experience the effects and the investors are not aware of the influence of mood on their decisions. Even if there is a mispricing (for example due to the changes in mood/weather effect), the mispricing can exist for a longer period (Barberis and Thaler, 2002). This also applies when the mispricing is caused by a small group of investors.

Schneider, Lesko and Garrett (1980) found that weather affects behavior, especially the interpersonal interactions. By analyzing the stock market, Shalen (1993) noticed that bad moods (caused for example by bad weather) lead to more disagreement among investors which causes higher volatility. Brown (1999) however argued that a good sentiment (good mood) leads to more trades and a higher volatility.

Psychology has shown that the weather (in different forms) can affect mood, which influences the behavior of investors. It is important to notice that the determinant factor is the occurrence of the weather itself and not the weather forecast (Hirshleifer and Shumway, 2003; Akhtari, 2011). Current weather affects mood and behavior, while mood and behavior are not affected by expectations about the weather (forecast).

2.2. Weather and the stock market

The literature connecting investor weather and stock market returns is differentiated based on the researched location. Saunders (1993) is the first one to investigate the United States market and find support for the influence of investors' mood – which is affected by weather - on asset prices. The study showed that the weather in New York City had a significant correlation with the daily returns on the NYSE and AMEX index over 1962-1989 and the Dow Jones Industrial Average over the period

1927-1989. The amount of cloud cover (used as a proxy for the inverse of sunshine) was negatively related to the returns on the stock market. Also, the results are robust to the inclusion of other market anomalies. Further, the effect of extreme weather on market returns is even larger.

In addition to this study, Chang, Chen, Chou and Li (2008) also found that the stock market returns on the NYSE on cloudy days are lower than on sunny days. However, the influence of the cloud cover is only significant at the opening of the market (12-15 minutes). The findings also show that weather has a significant influence on the intraday trading patterns. The cloud coverage is positively related to the volatility in the market and negatively related to the market depth. Akhtari (2011) investigated the relationship between weather and stock market returns over time. She also found a positive correlation between sunshine and stock market returns for New York City over the period 1948-2010 after controlling for market anomalies and seasonal effects. The author concluded that this connection is slightly increasing over the past half century. Loughran and Schultz (2004) also found evidence of lower stock returns on the Nasdaq on cloudy days. The weather in the neighborhood of companies' headquarters was, however, unrelated to the returns on the stocks of the companies.

However, the significance of the relationship is very much dependent on the period that is considered under the study. There are clear cyclical patterns visible in the weather effect. One possible explanation for the cyclical patterns is the emergence of non-rational investors in the stock market during certain periods in time - for instance for periods when investing in the stock market is popular. While less professional and, arguably, less rational investors enter the market, equity mispricing will occur more often (Akhtari, 2011).

In order to check if the weather effect is present globally, Hirshleifer and Shumway (2003) conducted a study investigating the influence of cloud cover in the morning (when the market opens) on 26 international stock markets for the period 1982-1997. The authors also found a significant negative relationship between cloud coverage and equity returns. Almost 70% of the countries showed a negative coefficient of cloud coverage on returns. When controlling for the cloudiness, snow and rain were not significantly related to market returns. Nonetheless, the authors conclude that it is very difficult to use trading strategies based on the weather effect. This requires frequent trading that can only be profitable when transactions costs are low and benefits are larger than these costs.

Cao and Wei (2005) investigated the link between temperature and the returns on nine stock indices around the world. The research observed a robust significant negative correlation between temperature and stock market returns for all globally dispersed countries. This relationship was stronger in winter than in summer. The impact of temperature on stock market returns was also more important than the influence of sunshine and the length of the night. Symeonidis, Daskalakis and Markellos (2011) focused on the influence of weather (cloudiness, temperature, precipitation and nighttime length) on the volatility of globally dispersed stock markets. In general, cloud coverage and the length of nighttime were significant and negatively related to stock market returns. However, the results proved to be depended on the location of focus.

The aforementioned studies have a found significant relationship between weather and stock market returns or market volatility. However, these studies were focused on the United States or multiple countries at once. Floros (2011) found a negative connection between temperature and stock market returns for Portugal. Sriboonchitta, Chitip, Sriwichailampham and Chaiboonsri (2011) came to the same conclusion for the stock market in Thailand. Keef and Roush (2002) found only a small significant relationship between stock market returns and temperature in New Zealand and no significant relationship between cloud coverage and returns. On the other hand, wind had a strong significant influence. Dowling and Lucey (2005) concluded that rain, lunar phases, daylight time and seasonal fluctuations are all significant and negatively related to equity returns on the Irish stock market. They did not find support for the impact of cloud cover and humidity. Kaustia and Rantapuska (2011) supports the influence of lunar phases (positive), daylight (negative), precipitation (negative) and sunlight (positive) on the return and volume of the Finnish stock market, while no support was discovered for the seasonal affective disorder (SAD) and temperature.

Chang, Nieh, Yang and Yang (2006) investigated the influence of temperature, humidity and cloud coverage on the stock market in Taiwan. The authors concluded that temperature and cloud coverage had the strongest negative effect on the stock returns. The findings in the paper of Shu (2008) partially support this result. This study found evidence for the argument that weather influences the mood of investors, which influences the behavior of investors and thus the stock prices. Better weather (here defined as low temperature, low humidity and high barometric pressure) leads to higher stock returns in Taiwan. Nonetheless, the relationship is stronger for individual investors than for institutional investors. Lee and Wang (2011) also found that cloud coverage had a strong negative significant impact on the Taiwanese stock market, especially in low cloud cover periods.

Kang, Jiang, Lee and Yoon (2010) found strong results for the weather effect in Shanghai. The stock market in Shanghai allows trading of two distinct categories of stocks: A-shares and B-shares. A-shares are for domestic investors only and B-shares can be traded by foreign investors. The underlying idea of this study is that domestic investors are more affected by the weather (measured as temperature, humidity and sunshine) than foreign investors. The results show that over the whole period the weather effect is only significant for the A-shares; however, when the B-share market was opened for domestic investors the weather effect became also significant for B-shares. The same pattern applies for the volatility of the stock market. Yoon and Kang (2009) found mixed results for the Korean stock market. The influence of temperature, cloud cover and humidity has weakened over time because of the increased efficiency. In addition, the effect of extreme weather has been found strongly significant. These results are only valid before the Asian crisis of 1997. Weather is insignificant thereafter with respect to stock market returns.

Moreover, there is no general consensus in prior research about the significance of the weather effect on the stock market. Trombley (1997) was amongst the first to confront the results of Saunders (1993) with new evidence. The paper shows that the relationship between the weather and the stock market in New York City is less clear and strong than presented by Saunders. The weather effect is not present for the period before 1962 and the effect is not systematic throughout the year. Therefore, the author deems Saunders' conclusions as exaggerated. Krämer and Runde (1997) replicated the study of Saunders for the German market and found no significant systematic relationship between the weather and the stock market. According to the paper, the outcome of such a research depend strongly on the manner in which hypotheses are phrased, weather variables are defined and the type of test statistics to be used. The authors conclude that this type of research is more or less exposed to a form of data mining.

Furthermore, Gerlach (2007) argues that none of the weather effects (generated by e.g. rain, temperature) in the United States occur on trading days on which no macroeconomic announcements were made (more than 60% of the sample in the paper). The study provides support for the argument that macroeconomic announcements are the actual cause of stock price movements while the weather effect was coincidentally discovered to be significant on the days of macroeconomic events. These findings are in line with the efficient market hypothesis. Goetzmann and Zhu (2003) find no evidence for the influence of weather on the trading behavior for the individual trading accounts of investors (the data consists of over 80,000 investor accounts from the US). Pardo and Valor (2003) addressed the influence of sunshine and humidity on the returns of the stock market in Madrid. The paper used two different periods in time: a period with an open 'outcry' trading system and a period with the current computerized trading system. The authors found no support for the influence of sunshine and humidity on stock returns under both trading systems. Tufan and Hamarat (2004) discovered that cloudiness is not related with the stock market index of Istanbul. Instead, they found support for the weak form of efficiency.

Also, the returns on the Australian stock market are not significantly influenced by the weather (Worthington, 2006). No support has been found for the relationship between eleven weather variables and the stock market returns. The author noticed, however, that when the weather effect is not systematic at the market level individual investors might still be affected by weather. Levy and Galili (2008) concluded that cloudiness had no significant influence on the behavior of the average investor on the Israeli stock market. Nevertheless, the weather effect is significant for individual accounts of young men with low incomes. Yuksel and Yuksel (2009) studied the effect of temperature on daily stock market returns around the world. The authors concluded that the relationship is not spurious, but it is weaker as previously thought. Lu and Chou (2012) investigated the Shanghai stock exchange. The paper concluded that returns are unaffected by changes in the mood of investors caused by the weather (cloud coverage, temperature, humidity, precipitation and visibility). However, trading activities (market turnover, liquidity and volatility) are correlated with weather.

Kamstra, Kramer and Levy (2003) focused their research on the seasonal affective disorder (SAD). SAD is linked with the hours of daylight: the less hours of daylight, the higher the chance of depression. Psychology showed that this leads to more risk aversion. The authors found that SAD has a strong negative correlation with stock market returns for a global sample of nine countries. However, weather variables like cloud coverage, precipitation and temperature had no significant effect on the stock market. In a global research on the effect of weather on stock returns, Jacobsen and Marquering (2008) found little evidence to support the influence of temperature and SAD on the stock market. According to the authors, most studies use data-driven inference based on spurious correlations. As a consequence, they consider that it is premature to conclude that stock returns are influenced by changes in the mood of investors caused by the weather.

Despite the rich literature regarding this subject, as far as we are concerned no research has been conducted in order to investigate the different manner in which weather affects stock returns in developed and emerging countries. The starting point of our research question lies within previous studies examining market segmentation. A segmented market is equivalent with numerous local investors activating on the stock exchange while foreign participation in the local market is limited (Bekaert and Harvey, 1998). Previous studies have shown that market segmentation tends to be much larger for emerging countries than for developed markets (Korajczyk, 1996). Undoubtedly, local investors are more exposed to local conditions - and weather implicitly. Hence, following this flow of reasoning we would expect a stronger impact of weather variables on the returns on emerging stock markets relative to developed ones.

However, a smaller scale of this type of investigation has been performed in countries with dual classes of common equity. Kang *et al.* (2010) study the weather impact on restricted equity. They consider A-shares that can be held by domestic investors only and B-shares that are mainly in possession of foreign investors. Their results yield that the weather effect exists in A-shares only, thus supporting the idea that the weather effect manifests differently depending on market segmentation.

Also, most of the abovementioned studies support the idea that the relationship between weather and stock returns is more likely to be significant in emerging countries rather than in developed ones. Researchers found a significant and strong connection between the weather variables and returns in developing countries such as Thailand, Taiwan, China, Korea, whereas little or no evidence was discovered in New Zeeland, Germany, Spain and Australia. There are also mixed results for the United States, Ireland, Finland and Turkey that are counterintuitive with our expectations, further emphasizing the necessity of a research that studies distinctly emerging and developed countries.

2.3. Two decades of weather effect literature: a lack of consensus

The literature on the weather effect fails to converge towards a unique systematic and robust relationship between the weather and the stock market. Based on prior literature, it must be noticed that there are multiple potential causes for this lack of consensus.

Firstly, time might be a significant factor to be considered. Chang *et al.* (2008) showed that the impact of weather variable is only significant at the opening of the market. Akhtari (2011) discovered that the investigated relationship is not only dependent on the hour of the day, but also on the moment in time. Moreover, the weather effect has a cyclical pattern over the years. Trombley (1997) and Lee and Wang (2011) found that the effect is also varying throughout the year. Secondly, location is paramount. Keef and Roush (2002) argue that the effect of different weather variables depends on the specific location. This is supported by the paper of Symeonidis *et al.* (2011). Therefore, the different conclusions of similar researches might be explained by the wide variety of variables and locations. Nonetheless, Hirshleifer and Shumway (2003) found significant universal effects on average. Thirdly, the definitions and hypotheses used are crucial. The way in which the null hypothesis is formulated and the definitions are used have a large impact on the final conclusions (Krämer and Runde, 1997). Moreover, the type of investors considered is essential. Levy and Galili (2008) and Shu (2008) showed that the significance of the weather effect depends on the type of investors (average versus individuals). Finally, the procedure and test statistics might yield biased results (Krämer and Runde, 1997; Trombley, 1997).

Overall, the significance of the weather effect depends on time, location, definitions of weather, hypotheses formulation, investor type, the procedure and test statistic used in the research.

3. Data description

3.1. Data collection

In order to investigate the relationship between stock returns – the explained variable, and weather – the explanatory variables, two datasets are required. Daily data is used for 16 years over the period 1996-2011. This time span accounts for two issues we have encountered. First, all stock markets in both emerging and developed countries have been continuously trading within this period. Secondly, this time spans provides heterogeneity and eliminates a potential sample bias by inclusion of both expansion and crisis periods. Therefore, our data contains stock market crashes such as the Asian crisis, the Dotcom bubble and the Subprime crisis and Euro crisis.

For a balanced comparison, our analysis includes 10 developed and 10 emerging stock markets. In order to provide a consistent classification of the countries within a category, we use MSCI, FTSE and S&Ps criteria. This criterion includes quantitative benchmarks for stock market capitalization, market breadth and depth, but also qualitative factors such as restrictions to foreign investors, efficient market infrastucture etc. Our research encompasses the main stock market in the following developed countries: Australia, Canada, France, Germany, Japan, Netherlands, Norway, United Kingdom and the United States. The emerging stock markets considered are: Brazil, China, Czech Republic, India, Malaysia, Mexico, Poland, Russia, South Africa and Turkey.

We choose the stock market index that is best available and has the largest number of stocks included – the appendix can be consulted on further information about stock market indices per country. Daily stock indices are retrieved from Datastream. The total return index is preferred to the price index given the fact that the former mentioned includes dividends and eliminates a potential bias and undervaluation of the equity index. However, due to data availability, we use the price index for four countries: China, India, Mexico and Turkey. Log returns are computed following the formula:

$$\text{Log return} = \log (TR_t/TR_{t-1}) \tag{1}$$
$$\text{, where TR = total return index.}$$

However, it is surprising that most authors investigating the weather effect do not use the total return index in their research. Akhtari (2010), Saunders (1993), Worthington, (2006) and others examine the price index instead of the total return, which could lead to a potentially biased dataset and erroneous results.

We consider six weather variables: cloud cover (SKC), temperature (TEMP), sea level pressure (SLP), visibility (VISIB), wind speed rate (WIND) and precipitation (PRECP). Previous studies (Lu and Chou, 2012; Shu, 2008; Worthington, 2006) provide a solid background for inclusion of the aforementioned variables, even though they have never been studied alltogether. Moreover, the SKC is amongst the most reserached variable, with most influence on stock returns. The meteorological data is retrieved from the National Climate Data Center (NCDC: http://www.ncdc.noaa.gov/oa/ncdc.html). NCDC provides reliable datasets of best quality. Data collection involves the following steps:

1. A weather station is chosen based on data availability and proximity to the location of the stock exchange (appendix, table 20).
2. SKC, SLP, TEMP and WIND are retrieved as hourly data, whereas VISIB and PRECP are only available as daily data. This approach ensures a better measurement due to the fact that stock exchanges have specific opening hours.
3. There is a relative small number of missing values – under 0.5% for developed countries and less than 1% for emerging countries. Instead of being removed, these have been replaced with the last recorded variable; given the high frequency of data and additional alteration that will be applied to the variables, further research will not be affected by means of accounting for missing values.
4. Hourly data is transformed into daily data by averaging the variables within the particular trading hours of each stock exchange. Also, we add an extra dimension for this. Motivated by the study of Chang *et al.* (2008) that observe that the weather effect is more significant at the opening hours of the stock exchange and by psychological research that claims that people decide whether they are optimistic when they wake up and are already influenced by weather in the morning (Watson, 2000), we take into consideration an extra hour (or half an hour) before the opening of the market.

By definition, SKC denotes the fraction of the total celestial dome covered by clouds or other obscuring phenomena. This is measured in oktas and ranges from 0 to 8, where 0 means no cloud cover and 8 is the maximum cloud cover. We expect an inverse relationship between SKC and stock returns since a higher degree of cloudiness induces less optimism, hence a worsening investor mood and lower returns. TEMP is equivalent to air temperature and is measured in 'Celsius. Previous studies show that temperature has most influence on risk taking behavior if it records extreme values (Mehra and Sah, 2002). Therefore, we anticipate that excess temperature will have a negative influence on returns. SLP is the air pressure relative to mean sea level and is measured in hectopascals. High pressure is associated with good weather, hence the stock returns should increase. WIND represents the wind speed rate, the rate of horizontal travel of air past a fixed point measured in meters per second. Higher wind speeds would aggravate the individuals' mood and stock returns should be lower. VISIB is the visibility for the day in miles and it should influence returns in the same manner as SKC. PRECP is the rain and/or melted snow during the day in inches and hundredths. Higher precipitation should induce lower stock returns.

Weather variables are highly seasonal. In summer, the temperature, precipitation and wind are on average higher than in winter. In order to avoid spurious regressions, all weather variables are deseasonalized. As a means of robustness check, we provide two different means of deseasonalizing. Section 4 presents the results by using a seasonal adjustment method identical to Hirshleifer and Schumway (2003). First, we compute the average of each week for each year in every location. Then, we determine the average for each week of the year using the 16 year sample (resulting 53 averages) and then subtracted this from the daily variable, giving the excess variable. In addition, by using excess variables we take into consideration the unexpected component of weather change.

Section 5 shows the results by accounting for some criticism brought to Hirshleifer and Schumway (2003) seasonal adjustment method. We follow a similar procedure, but we do not provide an average for the entire sample (resulting 53*16 averages). This means of seasonal adjustment mitigates the following potential problems: changing weather averages over time as a result of global warming and differences across countries located in different climate zones. Compared to the seasonal adjustment procedure used by Hirshleifer and Schumway (2003), we do not seek to find a average for each week of the year using the 16 year sample. Averaging all weeks over our time sample introduces a look-ahead bias into the analysis. As of the first week of January of 1996, no person could perfectly forecast January weather patterns for the future 16 years. Investors care about the weather at the precise actual moment in time, and not about future forecasts. However, a potential issue with deseasonalizing is that investors do not perceive weather based on a seasonal pattern. Individuals do no consider yearly trends and averages, but simply judge whether a particular day has good weather conditions – if it is sunny, rainy, windy, cold or not. This supports the second method of deseasonalizing.

Moreover, our aim is to identify the exclusive influence of weather on stock returns. Therefore, in order to cater for the unspecified explanatory variables and macroeconomic events that impact stock exchanges globally we provide a differentiated treatment for outliers. We define outliers according to Hampel (2011) as the values that exceed the following interval:

[median – 5.2*median absolute deviation ; median + 5.2*median absolute deviation]   (2)
,where mean absolute deviation=median(|variable-median(variable)|).

Identified outliers are bounded to the minimum, respectively the maximum value of this interval. By applying this procedure we avoid misidentification of a significant weather influence on stock returns when in fact stock price movements are caused by macroeconomic events such as the crisis destabilizations or expansions excessive returns. Censoring the returns in this manner also balances the data to account for the criticism that Gerlach (2007) formulated against the weather effect. On the other hand, weather variables will not be censored since our purpose is to quantify the impact of extreme weather as well since severe weather conditions have been linked by previous literature with investors' mood and behavior (Bell, 1976).

3.2. Data analysis

The following section provides a statistical analysis of the data that will be further used in our empirical approach. Table 1 presents the descriptive analysis of the daily stock returns over the period 1996-2011. It reports raw log returns, whereas we proceed in following sections using censored data. However, censoring is only applied to excessive returns which account for approximately 3% of the total observations. The table shows that the average daily returns are very similar between countries, with the exception of Turkey. As expected, emerging countries have higher returns and standard deviations than developed countries. Thus, developing countries are riskier and more volatile. This can also be observed by analyzing the minimum, maximum, skewness and kurtosis. Volatility and extreme values are determined chiefly by the expansion and crisis periods that we have included in our sample.

Table 1: An overview of the descriptive statistics of daily raw returns of each index for each country. The log returns is calculated $R_t = \text{Log}(TR_t/TR_{t-1})$, where TR is the total return index. The mean, median, standard deviation, kurtosis, skewness, minimum and maximum are reported for the log returns. The analyzed period is 1996-2011.

	Mean	Median	Standard Deviation	Kurtosis	Skewness	Minimum	Maximum
Developed Countries							
Australia	0.0003	0.0003	0.0103	6.0445	-0.4024	-0.0876	0.0602
Canada	0.0003	0.0006	0.0116	8.8855	-0.6966	-0.0976	0.0937
France	0.0003	0.0003	0.0139	5.1711	-0.0772	-0.0926	0.1022
Germany	0.0002	0.0007	0.0158	4.1513	-0.1124	-0.0887	0.1080
Italy	0.0002	0.0003	0.0149	4.7061	-0.0697	-0.0862	0.1074
Japan	-0.0001	0.0000	0.0136	6.4572	-0.2793	-0.1001	0.1286
Netherlands	0.0002	0.0006	0.0143	5.3944	-0.2291	-0.0945	0.0983
Norway	0.0003	0.0007	0.0142	6.1229	-0.6362	-0.0971	0.0919
United Kingdom	0.0002	0.0003	0.0130	7.4098	-0.2152	-0.0946	0.1096
United States	0.0002	0.0004	0.0116	6.0255	-0.2173	-0.0871	0.0881
Average	0.0002	0.0004	0.0133	6.0368	-0.2935		
Emerging countries							
Brazil	0.0006	0.0003	0.0215	13.4779	0.3033	-0.1723	0.2882
China	0.0003	0.0000	0.0171	5.0745	-0.2345	-0.1044	0.0940
Czech Republic	0.0002	0.0000	0.0139	46.2156	-0.7463	-0.2381	0.2222
India	0.0004	0.0003	0.0168	5.4397	-0.2240	-0.1194	0.1549
Malaysia	0.0001	0.0000	0.0142	53.5672	0.4717	-0.2415	0.2082
Mexico	0.0006	0.0004	0.0154	6.8657	0.0307	-0.1431	0.1215
Poland	0.0004	0.0001	0.0149	3.5275	-0.3116	-0.1029	0.0789
Russia	0.0005	0.0003	0.0129	6.0439	-0.4537	-0.1269	0.0742
South Africa	0.0007	0.0005	0.0274	7.7803	-0.4495	-0.2120	0.2020
Turkey	0.0012	0.0002	0.0259	5.4927	-0.0180	-0.1998	0.1777
Average	0.0005	0.0002	0.0180	15.3485	-0.1632		

Table 2 shows the daily mean of the all weather variables. This table reports the raw meteorological data statistics before adjusting for seasonality. Excess variables are closer to an average of 0. Unlike the return variables, there are large differences in the world regarding all weather variables – mainly due to location and climate. The precipitation is higher in developed countries because of the location of these countries – on average they are situated in the Northern hemisphere, whereas emerging countries are spread in both hemispheres. This also applies to temperature - that is on average higher for emerging countries. Further, the median, standard deviation, kurtosis, skewness, minimum and maximum are also reported for each weather variable (consult appendix, table 21 until 26).

Table 2: An overview of the mean of all the daily raw weather variables over the period 1996-2011, precipitation (PRECP), sky cloud clover (SKC), sea level pressure (SLP), temperature in Celsius (TEMP), visibility (VISIB) and wind speed rate (WIND). PRECP is the rain and/or melted snow during the day in inches and hundredths. It has a 0 or at least 0. SKC is ranging from 0 to 8. SKC is measured in oktas. SKC denotes the fraction of the total celestial dome covered by clouds or other obscuring phenomena. SLP is the air pressure relative to mean sea level. This is measured in hectopascals. TEMP is measured in Celsius for the air temperature. VISIB is the visibility for the day in miles. WIND is the wind speed rate, the rate of horizontal travel of air past a fixed point.

	PRECP	SKC	SLP	TEMP	VISIB	WIND
Developed Countries						
Australia	0.0967	4.0082	10175.3242	17.1118	8.243	48.2791
Canada	0.0711	3.3838	10163.3949	7.9650	7.867	44.7828
France	0.0674	5.6436	10164.5543	13.4846	6.698	48.3625
Germany	0.0533	5.5858	10165.4152	12.8401	6.228	36.2542
Italy	0.0773	4.1244	10157.5321	16.6539	4.999	19.1246
Japan	0.1691	5.1803	10136.1433	17.2404	9.106	35.0921
Netherlands	0.0923	5.4190	10151.3863	12.1537	8.714	54.1246
Norway	1.4846	5.6342	10115.4958	6.9109	8.218	30.5429
United Kingdom	0.0661	5.2411	10151.0168	12.8643	8.514	44.5014
United States	0.1341	5.1188	10165.7412	12.0863	9.007	45.4153
Average	0.2312	4.9339	10154.6004	12.9311	7.7595	40.6480
Emerging countries						
Brazil	0.0870	5.2002	10212.7400	21.0037	6.560	29.9649
China	0.1247	4.6815	10166.1584	17.3891	10.318	31.2067
Czech Republic	0.0526	5.4243	10165.9253	11.5127	13.131	27.4063
India	0.2608	3.2524	10079.4725	29.4436	2.301	24.2171
Malaysia	0.2829	6.9980	10093.5346	28.4727	6.579	19.2021
Mexico	0.0873	3.4817	10095.8176	15.8095	6.559	22.1179
Poland	0.0627	5.3976	10157.9367	9.9294	6.896	39.8456
Russia	0.0119	5.7763	10155.5120	6.4480	20.953	29.1543
South Africa	0.0854	3.1342	10188.75	19.4972	7.481	41.7257
Turkey	0.0653	3.6944	10162.2810	16.7529	6.148	51.6680
Average	0.1121	4.7041	10147.8128	17.6259	8.6927	31.6509

4. Methodology and results

The purpose of our empirical investigation is to study the difference in the weather effect between developed and emerging countries. We approach this question by analyzing individual regressions for each city to examine if weather has a significant influence on the selected stock markets, then we proceed to pooled regressions to account for individual heterogeneity and make a clear separation between developed and emerging countries. Further, a logit model is employed to investigate the influence of weather on the probability of recording a positive, respectively a negative return and to determine the marginal effects of weather variables on stock market returns.

Since Saunders (1993), the most frequently used method to investigate the weather effect on stock returns is the ordinary least squares (OLS) regression model. Akhtari (2011), Hirshleifer and Shumway (2003), Dowling and Lucey (2005) and other studies examine the existence of the weather effect based on OLS regression. Other methods that have been used cater for the ARCH effects and include different GARCH models: GJR-GARCH (Kang *et al.*, 2010), AR-GARCH (Sriboonchitta *et al.*, 2011), ARMA-GARCH Worthington (2006) etc. Our study requires a focus on stock returns and not on volatility, hence the OLS procedure is most suitable. Even though we identify the presence of heteroskedasticity, this is corrected by using heteroskedasticity consistent standard errors so our inference still holds.

In addition to the six weather variables, our regression includes a one-day lagged stock return. This dynamic structure allows us to conclude upon the efficiency of the stock market and to account for the autocorrelation of the error terms. Prior literature provides further motivation for including an autoregressive structure of stock returns. Saunders (1993) uses the lagged return $R_{i,t-1}$ to account for the non-synchronous trading effects. Cao and Wei (2003) also incorporate the $R_{i,t-1}$ to correct the first order autocorrelations. Akhtari (2010) uses $R_{i,t-1}$ to control price movement persistence.

Moreover, in order to reduce the sources of omitted variables and to account for a pure effect of weather we include two dummy variables, one for the January effect and one for the Monday effect. Lakonishok and Smidt (1988), Jaffe and Westerfield (1985), Haugen and Philippe (1996) investigated various calendar effects and found significant results for month-of-the-year effect and day-of-the-week effect. Also, authors that studied the weather effect use dummies for calendar effects to control the results of the weather impact. Saunders (1993) uses dummy variables for the January effect and the Monday effect. Goetzmann and Zhu (2003) and Akhatari (2011) control these effects as well. Further, Cao and Wei (2005), Dowling and Lucey and Tufan and Hamarat (2004) control for the Monday effect. Other authors cater for these effects in a different manner. For instance, Cao and Wei (2005) and Kamstra *et al.* (2003) used the tax loss selling as a dummy.

4.1. City-by-city tests

So as to avoid spurious regressions, both stock returns and weather data is checked for stationarity. This ensures that our series have a constant mean, variance and autocovariance regardless of the moment of maesurement. We implement both the Augmented Dickey-Fuller and Phillips-Perron procedure that test under the null hypothesis if the series has a unit root, with the difference that Phillips-Perron test is robust to heteroskedasticity and error term autocorrelation. The statistics reject the null hypothesis for every series for a confidence level of over 99%, concluding that the data is stationary.

Before presenting the final results of the OLS regressions, we proceed with employing specific tests in order to examine if our regressions are consistent with the classical linear model assumptions. All tests are performed and inference is built by setting a 1% significance level and results are reported in table 3. First, homoskedasticity is analyzed by using the Breusch-Godfrey-Pagan test with the null hypothesis of constant variance of error tems. For each of the 20 regressions this hypothesis is rejected for a confidence level of 99% (the F-statistics of the test is shown in the table 3), which implies that the resulting coefficients are inefficient. Error terms autocorrelation is further investigated with the aid of Breusch-Godfrey test with the null hypothesis of independent errors. The number of lagged residuals that are included in the residual test equation are selected based on the minimum Akaike Information Criterion. Most residual series are correlated with a one-day lagged value, while the maximum number of lags is 5 – a conservative number given the frequency of the data. The results of the test show that most countries comply with error term independence assumption, even though results vary from state to state.

Depending on the results of the aforementioned tests, we use heteroskedasticity and autocorrelation consistent standard errors in order to draw correct inference on the significance of the variables. If these tested assumptions of the linear model are violated, coefficients remain unbiased and consistent while losing efficiency. This is corrected by using either White standard errors in the presence of heteroskedasticity and Newey and West (1987) variance-covariance estimators in the presence of both heteroskedasticity and autocorrelation. Therefore, the estimated values of the coefficients are on average equal to their true values and significance is examined on an efficient basis.

Moreover, normality is examined by the use of the Jarque-Bera test with the null hypothesis of normal error distribution. The Jarque-Bera statistic is reported in table 3. Given a 1% significance level, none of the residual series comply with this assumption since most of them are leptokurtic even though they are symmetrical. These results are consistent with the fat tails of the series and the fact that the sample includes a profusion of both positive and negative events that induce extreme values. However, viola-

16

tion of this assumption is virtually inconsequential for our analysis considering the large sample we selected.

Finally, explanatory variable multicollinearity is tested. Hence, we construct the correlogram for each of the 20 countries and report the variables with the maximum correlation coefficient in table 3. For a rule of thumb correlation benchmark of 80%, we conclude that the weather variables are not collinear and can be used altogether in individual regressions.

Table 3: The test performed in order to check for OLS assumptions with the Hirshleifer and Schumway(2003) deseasonalizing data. These are performed under a 99% confidence level and we report the corresponding statistics. For the correlogram, the maximum correlation coefficient is reported and the variables that are associated to this coefficient. For the Breusch-Godfrey test the number of lags is chosen by minimizing the Akaike Information Criterion. The '√' is equivalent to compliance with the OLS assumption, whereas the 'X' represents a violation of the OLS assumption.

	Breusch-Pagan-Godfrey		Breusch-Godfrey				Jarque-Bera		Correlogram		
	Homoskedasticity		Autocorrelation				Normality		Multicollinearity		
	F-statistic		F-statistic	Lags	min AIC		JB statistic		Max corr	Variables	
Developed countries											
Australia	23.7950	X	2.8167	2	-6.5134	X	161.8924	X	0.3245	PRECP-SKC	√
Canada	2.7997	X	2.7997	2	-7.7353	√	354.7240	X	-0.3997	SLP-SKC	√
France	8.4574	X	4.1034	3	-5.9107	X	176.4726	X	-0.3205	SLP-SKC	√
Germany	10.6383	X	2.6576	4	-5.6320	√	157.2800	X	-0.2847	SKC-VISIB	√
Italy	6.4800	X	5.2519	4	-5.7678	X	136.4723	X	-0.4339	SKC-TEMP	√
Japan	6.5979	X	2.6800	3	-5.9401	X	95.8786	X	-0.4950	SKC-VISIB	√
Netherlands	11.1562	X	4.1472	5	-5.8906	X	186.1127	X	0.2389	PRECP-WIND	√
Norway	11.7289	X	0.2945	2	-5.9126	√	183.9669	X	-0.2749	SKC-VISIB	√
UK	7.3172	X	6.5888	4	-6.2960	X	171.1813	X	-0.4653	SLP-PRECP	√
US	4.0892	X	2.2517	2	-6.1165	√	140.2803	X	-0.3075	PRECP-VISIB	√
Emerging countries											
Brazil	13.4782	X	1.9440	3	-5.0821	√	167.2561	X	-0.3976	SKC-TEMP	√
China	7.4434	X	7.3750	4	-5.5705	X	136.9589	X	-0.5970	SLP-TEMP	√
Czech Republic	9.2394	X	1.3938	2	-6.1649	√	178.7923	X	0.4571	VISIB-WIND	√
India	10.7022	X	0.5654	2	-5.5164	√	195.8421	X	-0.2866	SKC-TEMP	√
Malaysia	9.2968	X	9.2968	3	-6.4514	√	164.9247	X	0.5672	SLP-TEMP	√
Mexico	5.4487	X	4.7759	2	-5.7270	√	152.9068	X	-0.4909	SLP-TEMP	√
Poland	6.4182	X	1.5562	2	-5.7113	√	130.4603	X	0.2427	VISIB-WIND	√
Russia	4.3424	X	0.9387	2	-4.7000	√	143.1389	X	0.3529	SLP-VISIB	√
South Africa	5.1734	X	5.3055	3	-6.0426	X	185.2629	X	-0.5412	SKC-TEMP	√
Turkey	4.7109	X	3.5776	5	-6.1361	X	362.5465	X	-0.3202	SKC-VISIB	√

Based on the abovementioned test results and corrections, we proceed with presenting the results of city-by-city regressions. We estimate the following model for each individual country:

$$R_{it} = \alpha_{it} + \beta_{l1}R_{i,t-1} + \beta_{l2}PRECP_{it} + \beta_{l3}SKC_{it} + \beta_{l4}SLP_{it} + \beta_{l5}TEMP_{it} + \beta_{l6}VISIB_{it} + \beta_{l7}WIND_{it} + \beta_{l8}DJAN_{it} + \beta_{l9}DMON_{it} + \varepsilon_{it} \quad (3)$$

, where R is the stock return, PRECP is precipitation, SKC is sky cloud cover, SLP is sea level pressure, TEMP is air temperature, VISIB is visibility, WIND is wind speed, DJAN is a dummy variable for the January effect, DMON is a dummy variable for the Monday effect, α is a constant and ε is the error term that incorporates all other explanatory variables not mentioned by this model.

Table 4 displays the results of individual OLS regressions. These show heterogenity regarding both the value of the coefficients and their significance. Nonetheless, the lagged return is more frequently significant in emerging countries (6 emerging versus 0 developed countries), which means that stock returns in emerging countries are further away from the random walk hypothesis of efficient markets. On average, we can conclude that emerging countries are less efficient than developed countries. In addition to this, the Monday effect is present in 7 of the 10 emerging countries we analyzed, whereas none of the developed countries show a significant Monday effect. Based on the negative coefficients for all developing countries, returns on Monday tend to be lower in emerging countries, while developed countries do not exhibit any pattern or a statistical difference between Monday trading compared to the rest of the week. This is further proof of emerging markets being less efficient.

Furthermore, there is no systematic difference between emerging and developed countries in terms of weather variables. Also, significant weather variables differ from country to country, without persistance of one variable over more countries. Therefore, we cannot identify one weather variable to be the most important. Noteworthy, the sign of the significant coefficients coincides is not overall consistent with the expectations. We notice erratic patterns of the coefficients signs that are in disagreement with the anticipations. For instance, precipitation causes positive returns in 13 countries out of 20. This is counterintuitive and signals a potential loss of value when using this means of deseasonalizing. Table 5 presents an overview of the of the significant variables in emerging and developed countries.

Table 4: Results of the OLS regression model 1996-2011 with the Hirshleifer and Schumway(2003) deseasonalizing method. We report the estimates for each explanatory variable and in brackets we show the standard error of the estimators. Significance level: * (10%), ** (5%) and *** (1%). Scaled numbers by 100.

	α	Rt-1	PRECP	SKC	SLP	TEMP	VISIB	WIND	DJAN	DMON
Developed countries										
Australia	0.0421**	-2.2795	0.0143	0.0047	-0.0000	0.0010	0.0060	0.0001	-0.0561	0.0216
	(0.0164)	(1.8433)	(0.0437)	(0.0068)	(0.0002)	(0.0070)	(0.0082)	(0.0007)	(0.0460)	(0.0364)
Canada	0.0156*	0.0462	0.0410	-0.0050	0.0001	-0.0007	-0.0029	0.0002	0.0031	-0.0098
	(0.0090)	(3.1268)	(0.0510)	(0.0033)	(0.0001)	(0.0022)	(0.0054)	(0.0003)	(0.0272)	(0.0203)
France	0.0258	2.0269	0.0183	-0.0030	0.0001	0.0044	-0.0053	-0.0004	0.0055	-0.0067
	(0.0221)	(1.7109)	(0.1298)	(0.0101)	(0.0002)	(0.0051)	(0.0079)	(0.0012)	(0.0689)	(0.0497)
Germany	0.0269	-0.8243	-0.0187	0.0172*	0.0003	-0.0040	0.0027	-0.0001	-0.0180	0.0492
	(0.0271)	(1.9577)	(0.1313)	(0.0100)	(0.0003)	(0.0027)	(0.0187)	(0.0014)	(0.0783)	(0.0590)
Italy	0.0272	1.6034	0.0288	0.0029	0.0000	0.0157**	0.0092	0.0016	0.0470	-0.0370
	(0.0233)	(1.7268)	(0.0640)	(0.0105)	(0.0003)	(0.0073)	(0.0149)	(0.0018)	(0.0831)	(0.0539)
Japan	0.0018	2.6106	-0.0048	-0.0217	-0.0004	0.0063	0.0044	-0.0032	-0.0260	-0.0335
	(0.0211)	(1.6086)	(0.0305)	(0.0613)	(0.0015)	(0.0113)	(0.0128)	(0.0027)	(0.0685)	(0.0501)
Netherlands	0.0223	1.2396	0.1789*	-0.0027	0.0002	0.0080	0.0120***	0.0005	-0.0592	0.0598
	(0.0222)	(1.8204)	(0.1083)	(0.0091)	(0.0002)	(0.0055)	(0.0043)	(0.0008)	(0.0686)	(0.0512)
Norway	0.0587***	2.6886	0.0008	-0.0191*	-0.0002	-0.0031	0.0026	-0.0008	-0.0062	-0.0133
	(0.0224)	(2.0983)	(0.0012)	(0.0103)	(0.0002)	(0.0047)	(0.0044)	(0.0012)	(0.0721)	(0.0508)
UK	0.0475**	0.2351	-0.0228	0.0113	0.0000	0.0040	0.0035	-0.0005	-0.0951*	0.0108
	(0.0191)	(1.7836)	(0.1265)	(0.0082)	(0.0002)	(0.0054)	(0.0030)	(0.0009)	(0.0523)	(0.0416)
US	0.0336**	-4.6176	0.0156	-0.0005	0.0004*	-0.0019	0.0063	0.0007	-0.0469	0.0054
	(0.0206)	(1.9046)	(0.0563)	(0.0078)	(0.0003)	(0.0049)	(0.0101)	(0.0010)	(0.0619)	(0.0433)
Emerging countries										
Brazil	0.1060***	3.1689	0.1397	0.0028	-0.0003	0.0032	0.0049	0.0034	-0.0144	-0.1541**
	(0.0367)	(2.0439)	(0.1497)	(0.0143)	(0.0003)	(0.0083)	(0.0150)	(0.0023)	(0.1161)	(0.0765)
China	0.0198	-0.2402	-0.0296	0.0061	0.0005	-0.0001	-0.0023	-0.0030	0.0005	-0.1185*
	(0.0255)	(1.5975)	(0.0577)	(0.0093)	(0.0007)	(0.0098)	(0.0084)	(0.0019)	(0.0854)	(0.0622)
Czech Republic	0.0161	9.1773***	0.1395	-0.0031	0.0001	0.0020	0.0004	0.0022	0.0214	0.0228
	(0.0201)	(2.0669)	(0.1184)	(0.0086)	(0.0002)	(0.0042)	(0.0034)	(0.0015)	(0.0585)	(0.0435)
India	0.0264***	8.5436	0.0213	0.0214	0.0014	0.0155	-0.0216	0.0013	-0.1113	0.1137*
	(0.0270)	(2.0488)	(0.0296)	(0.0168)	(0.0012)	(0.0122)	(0.0231)	(0.0020)	(0.0892)	(0.0647)
Malaysia	0.0204	16.3707***	-0.0134	0.0210	-0.0000	0.0090	-0.0134	-0.0037	0.0689	-0.1528***
	(0.0188)	(2.1319)	(0.0261)	(0.0472)	(0.0000)	(0.0112)	(0.0137)	(0.0023)	(0.0559)	(0.0380)
Mexico	0.0683**	11.0986***	-0.0161	0.0058	0.0002	0.0029	0.0023	0.0002	-0.0407	-0.0942*
	(0.0265)	(1.6487)	(0.0900)	(0.0079)	(0.0004)	(0.0030)	(0.0033)	(0.0016)	(0.0828)	(0.0538)
Poland	0.0029	11.6350***	0.0964	-0.0030	-0.0001	0.0078	-0.0105	-0.0017	0.1302*	0.0671
	(0.0260)	(1.5389)	(0.1255)	(0.0124)	(0.0003)	(0.0052)	(0.0090)	(0.0013)	(0.0778)	(0.0538)
Russia	0.0866*	12.9533***	0.9563	-0.0385**	0.0000	-0.0031	0.0108*	0.0018	-0.0516	0.1060
	(0.0442)	(2.0877)	(0.6368)	(0.0169)	(0.0004)	(0.0065)	(0.0057)	(0.0026)	(0.1328)	(0.0905)
South Africa	0.0256	7.5982***	-0.2008***	0.0121	0.0001	0.0070	-0.0040	-0.0014	0.0261	-0.1249***
	(0.0236)	(1.8129)	(0.0656)	(0.0118)	(0.0001)	(0.0069)	(0.00960)	(0.00140)	(0.0738)	(0.0465)
Turkey	0.0693***	2.6606	0.0612	0.0180*	0.0045	0.0130**	-0.0265	0.0003	0.0538	-0.1240***
	(0.0188)	(2.2049)	(0.0909)	(0.0095)	(0.0037)	(0.0066)	(0.0213)	(0.0010)	(0.0674)	(0.0462)

Table 5: An overview of the significant weather variables for each country over the period 1996-2011 with the Hirshleifer and Schumway(2003) deseasonalizing data. The significance level is set to 10% and less.

Developed		Emerging	
Australia	-	Brazil	-
Canada	-	China	-
France	-	Czech Republic	-
Germany	SKC	India	-
Italy	TEMP	Malaysia	-
Japan	-	Mexico	-
Netherlands	VISIB, PRECP	Poland	-
Norway	SKC	Russia	VISIB,SKC
UK	-	South Africa	PRECP
US	SLP	Turkey	TEMP

4.2. Joint tests

4.2.1. Pooled least squares regression

We address the issue of dispersed individual regression results by separating the countries into emerging and developed. So as to draw a conclusion regarding the different significance of the weather effect in developed and emerging countries we make use of a pooled regression of the following form:

$$R_{it} = \alpha + \beta_1 R_{i,t-1} + \beta_2 PRECP_{it} + \beta_3 SKC_{it} + \beta_4 SLP_{it} + \beta_5 TEMP_{it} + \beta_6 VISIB_{it} + \beta_7 WIND_{it} + \beta_8 DJAN_{it} + \beta_9 DMON_{it} + \varepsilon_{it} \quad (4)$$

,where α and β_n are the same for each country.

The data is comprised of three different categories of balanced panel data: world (all countries included in the sample), developed countries and emerging countries. Based on the previous data analysis, we assume that the error terms (ε_{it}) are independent and identically distributed (i.i.d.).

By using the Hausman test to check if our model better accommodates random or fixed effects, it can be concluded that there are cross-sectional random effects (p-value close to 1). Therefore, the constant (α) is uncorrelated with the explanatory variables (x_{it}). The heterogeneity in the cross-section part of the panel data is incorporated in the error term. Random effects are also more appropriate because the developed and emerging countries have been selected randomly from the population (Brooks, 2008). When observations are randomly taken out of the population, the correlation in the error terms for different observations is ruled out (Wooldridge, 2009). By using the random effects regression analysis, the model is also more parsimonious than when using the fixed effects model. White panel corrected standard errors are used to control for the contemporaneous covariance between the errors terms of the cross-section of countries over time.

Table 6 shows the results for the entire estimation period (1996-2011). The conclusion is more prominent than for individual regressions. First, the coefficients are modest for the explanatory weather variables. These identify visibility as the only significant variable for both emerging and developed countries. Thus, there is no difference in the weather effect between the two types of countries, conclusion that is reinforced by the fact that the overall analysis for the world is significant for visibility as well. A 100 unit increase in visibility over the world causes a 0.0046 percentage points increase in returns.

In addition to this, visibility has a positive coefficient, as anticipated. With respect to the other variables, cloud cover has a correct sign, precipitation and wind are not consistent with the common sens suggested coefficients, whereas pressure and temperature have different signs than expected for emerging countries.

Regarding markets efficiency, it can be observed that the lagged returns are highly significant for the emerging countries (99% confidence level), but insignificant for the developed countries. This indicates that returns can be partially predicted based on previous returns, which is not consistent with the random walk notion of the efficient market hypotheses. This finding is consistent with the results of the city-by-city tests.

Table 6: The results of pooled regressions for the period 1996-2011 with the Hirshleifer and Schumway(2003) deseasonalizing data. We report the estimates for each explanatory variable and in brackets we show the standard error of the estimators. Significance level: * (10%), ** (5%) and *** (1%). Scaled numbers by 100.

	α	R_{t-1}	PRECP	SKC	SLP	TEMP	VISIB	WIND	DJAN	DMON
World	0.0413***	5.3434***	0.0008	-0.0006	0.0000	-0.0000	0.0046***	0.0001	-0.0042	-0.0033
	(0.0145)	(0.8844)	(0.0012)	(0.0024)	(0.0000)	(0.0014)	(0.0015)	(0.0003)	(0.0449)	(0.0353)
Developed countries	0.0311*	0.7903	0.0006	-0.0006	0.0001	-0.0012	0.0044*	0.0002	-0.0252	0.0063
	(0.0159)	(1.2529)	(0.0012)	(0.0029)	(0.0001)	(0.0017)	(0.0022)	(0.0003)	(0.0467)	(0.0370)
Emerging countries	0.0517***	7.8088***	0.0102	-0.0002	-0.0000	0.0015	0.0046**	0.0001	0.0159	-0.0133
	(0.0154)	(0.9453)	(0.0190)	(0.0039)	(0.0000)	(0.0020)	(0.0020)	(0.0006)	(0.0507)	(0.0382)

In order to reconcile the lack of consensus of prior literature upon the weather effect generated by sample time difference, we divide our sample into different subsamples and check whether a pattern might emerge. We make use of both non-overlapping data that divides the sample into 5 periods of 3 years and overlapping data by using 14 different subsamples of 3 years length.

Table 7 reports the estimation of a similar model during time periods of three years. Based on these results, there is also no difference between the weather effect in developed countries and emerging countries. We cannot identify a distinct pattern regarding the recurrence of the weather effect, although a cyclical pattern might fit the results.

Table 7: Significant weather variables for the world (20 countries), the developed countries and the emerging countries for different periods in time within the total period 1996-2011 with the Hirshleifer and Schumway (2003) deseasonalizing data. OLS regression model is used. Weather variables confidence level is set to 90%.

	World	Developed countries	Emerging countries
1996-1998	SKC	WIND	TEMP
1999-2001	SKC,SLP	SKC,SLP	-
2002-2004	PRECP,VISIB	PRECP	SKC,TEMP
2005-2007	-	SKC	-
2008-2011	VISIB	-	VISIB

Further, overlapping time periods are used in order to investigate the significance of the weather variables over time and to identify a clearer pattern regarding the weather effect. Table 8 reports the results of 3 years rolling periods. These show that the weather effect displays a rather cyclical pattern, with periods where no weather variables are found significant, and periods where the weather effect is highly significant. Weather appears to be significant in periods such as 1996-1998, 1999-2001, 2002-2006 which largely correspond to economic expansion phases. After the burst of speculative bubbles, weather has no significant influence on investors's decisions.

In addition, a decreasing pattern emerges in terms of weather variables significance. We identify cloud cover and pressure to be the most important variables before the year 2001, within a confidence level of 99%, whereas cloud cover and visibility are the chief significant variables after 2002, but the confidence level decreases to 95%, respectively 90%. Also, after 2002 the other weather variables are significant within an expanded significance level. These results stand as proof as a diminishing influence of weather in time. However, a trade-off between the number of significant weather variables and their significance show that weather has a cyclical pattern over time.

Table 8: Significant weather variables for the world (20 countries), the developed countries and the emerging countries for rolling 3 year periods with the Hirshleifer and Schumway (2003) deseasonalizing data. OLS regression model. Weather variables confidence level is set to 90%.

	World	Developed countries	Emerging countries
1996-1998	SKC^{**}	$WIND^{**}$	$TEMP^{**}$
1997-1999	SKC^{***}	-	SKC^{***}
1998-2000	-	-	-
1999-2001	SKC^{**},SLP^{***}	SKC^{**},SLP^{***}	-
2000-2002	SKC^{***}	SKC^{***},SLP^{*}	$SKC^{***},TEMP^{*}$
2001-2003	-	-	-
2002-2004	$PRECP^{**},VISIB^{**}$	$PRECP^{**}$	$VISIB^{**}$
2003-2005	$VISIB^{**}$	SKC^{**}	$VISIB^{**}$
2004-2006	$TEMP^{*},WIND^{**}$	SKC^{**}	$SKC^{**},TEMP^{**},WIND^{*}$
2005-2007	-	SKC^{**}	-
2006-2008	-	-	-
2007-2009	$VISIB^{*}$	$VISIB^{*}$	$VISIB^{**}$
2008-2010	$VISIB^{*}$	$WIND^{*}$	$VISIB^{**}$
2009-2011	-	-	SKC^{*}

4.2.2. Binary regression

The previous pooled regressions related the level of returns to the level of the various weather variables on a particular day. While this method indicates that the sign of the return might be related to the weather in the country, the magnitude of the return might be differently related or not related to weather. The different weather variables can influence differently the probability of having positive returns. By using a logit model, we can check whether the weather in developed and emerging countries have a different influence on the probability of having particular positive or negative returns.

In addition, the logit model is a means of robustness check. We can verify if the sign of the weather variables coefficients are indeed the ones both common sense and previous papers anticipated. Also, weather influences mood and determines an optimistic or pessimistic approach of investors. Therefore, although weather might not influence the level of returns, it might induce a positive or negative trend on the market that is reflected by positive or negative returns. Moreover, this estimation allows us to infer upon the position an investor should take on the market.

For this model the log returns of the market are assigned the value '0' for negative or zero returns and the value '1' for a positive return - as used by Hirshleifer and Shumway (2003) and Loughran and Schultz (2004). The division of the returns between 0 and 1 is balanced, with a portion of positive log returns of 55.10% - world, 54.86% - developed countries and 55.35% - emerging countries. The following logistic model is estimated, where P is the probability that the returns are positive, by using maximum likelihood.

$$P(R_{it} > 0) = \frac{1}{1 + e^{-(\beta_1 PRECP_{it} + \beta_2 SKC_{it} + \beta_3 SLP_{it} + \beta_4 TEMP_{it} + \beta_5 VISIB_{it} + \beta_6 WIND_{it})}} \tag{5}$$

The results of this estimation are shown in table 9. These illustrate that the influence of weather on the magnitude of stock returns is higher than on the actual level of returns. Visbility is the only significant coefficient for developed countries, whereas temperature is significant for emerging countries. Based on these, we stress the idea of no difference in the weather effect between emerging and developed markets.

Table 9: Logit estimation of the probability of having a positive stock return over the period 1996-2011 for the world (20 countries), developed countries and emerging countries with the Hirshleifer and Schumway(2003) deseasonalizing data. Standard errors are reported between parentheses. Significance level: * (10%), ** (5%) and *** (1%).

	α	PRECP	SKC	SLP	TEMP	VISIB	WIND
World	0.2059***	0.0014	-0.0001	-0.0000	0.0003	0.0051**	-0.0004
	(0.0070)	(0.0026)	(0.0033)	(0.0000)	(0.0017)	(0.0020)	(0.0004)
Developed countries	0.1971***	0.0013	-0.0052	-0.0000	-0.0030	0.0068**	-0.0004
	(0.0100)	(0.0026)	(0.0046)	(0.0001)	(0.0023)	(0.0034)	(0.0005)
Emerging countries	0.2153***	0.0119	0.0063	-0.0000	0.0044*	0.0041	-0.0002
	(0.0099)	(0.0260)	(0.0048)	(0.0000)	(0.0024)	(0.0025)	(0.0007)

Neverthelss, the coefficients of the logit model do not reflect the direct influence upon the probability of recording positive or nagtive returns. Therefore, the marginal effects for each of the weather variables is estimated using the following formula:

$$\hat{P}(R_{it} > 0) = \frac{1}{1 + e^{-(\hat{\beta}_1 \overline{PRECP} + \hat{\beta}_2 \overline{SKC} + \hat{\beta}_3 \overline{SLP} + \hat{\beta}_4 \overline{TEMP} + \hat{\beta}_5 \overline{VISIB} + \hat{\beta}_6 \overline{WIND})}} \tag{6}$$

,where the mean values of the explanatory weather variables are used together with the coefficient estimates of the logit model so as to calculate the probability of positive returns. The marginal effects are computed by multiplying the coefficient estimates of the logit models with the probability (which is equal to the proportion of positive log returns).

Table 10 shows the marginal effects for the world, developed and emerging countries. Based on these findings, there is no indication of a significant difference in the magnitude of the weather effect between developed and emerging countries. On the other hand, the results confirm that weather has a limited and small impact on the returns of worldwide stock markets. For instance, a 1 unit increase in the visibility in developed countries causes a 0.0037 percentage points increase in stock returns. However, an accuracy check based on the correspondence of the coefficients signs shows mixed results. Visibility and wind are the only variables with a correct coefficient sign.

Table 10: Marginal effects for probability of an upward stock market by using the logit model, for the world (20 countries), developed countries and emerging countries with the Hirshleifer and Schumway (2003) deseasonalizing data.

	α	PRECP	SKC	SLP	TEMP	VISIB	WIND
World	0.1135	0.0008	-0.0001	-0.0000	0.0002	0.0028	-0.0002
Developed countries	0.1081	0.0007	-0.0029	-0.0000	-0.0017	0.0037	-0.0002
Emerging countries	0.1191	0.0066	0.0035	-0.0000	0.0024	0.0023	-0.0001

5. Robustness check

In order to check if our findings are consistent regardless of how the weather variables are deseasonalized, we apply a different means of seasonal adjustment. In this section, data is deseasonalized as follows: excess weather variables are computed by substracting the average of the week of the corresponding year. With the exception of the seasonal adjustment method, we keep the identical methodology followed in Section 4. City-by-city, panel and binary regressions are employed in order to conclude upon the accuracy of our conclusions. The findings of this section are similar with previous results; however, we identify a stronger significance concerning the weather effect.

5.1. City-by-city tests

The OLS regression model assumptions are checked again and results are presented in table 11. According to these, we employ White or HAC standard erros. Noteworhy, the correlations between the weather variables do not change much and they remain at moderate levels, implying that the excess variables using two different means of seasonal adjustment are comparable. Further, the results of individual regressions are presented in table 12.

Table 11: The test results for OLS assumptions for a different means of data deseazonalizing. These are performed under a 99% confidence level and we report the corresponding statistics. For the correlogram, the maximum correlation coefficient is reported and the variables that are associated to this coefficient. For the Breusch-Godfrey test the number of lags is chosen by minimizing the Akaike Information Criterion. The '√' is equivalent to compliance with the OLS assumption, whereas the 'X' represents a violation of the OLS assumption.

	Breusch-Pagan-Godfrey		Breusch-Godfrey				Jarque-Bera		Correlogram		
	Homoskedasticity		Autocorrelation				Normality		Multicollinearity		
	F-statistic		F-statistic	Lags	min AIC		JB statistic		Max corr	Variables	
Developed countries											
Australia	4.4361	X	0.9595	2	-6.5126	√	164.4440	X	-0.3921	PRECP-VISIB	√
Canada	3.3531	X	2.0747	2	-6.3538	√	234.9513	X	-0.3652	SLP-VISIB	√
France	7.3939	X	4.0895	3	-5.9135	X	173.6732	X	-0.3313	SLP-WIND	√
Germany	8.6094	X	2.4372	4	-5.6316	√	161.0347	X	0.2223	SKC-VISIB	√
Italy	8.2780	X	5.9344	5	-5.7730	X	139.0266	X	-0.5062	SKC-TEMP	√
Japan	3.7436	X	2.7689	3	-5.9414	√	98.8978	X	-0.4058	SKC-VISIB	√
Netherlands	8.8251	X	3.9987	5	-5.8883	X	189.5935	X	-0.3321	SLP-WIND	√
Norway	7.3715	X	1.0355	2	-5.9130	√	186.1579	X	-0.3626	SKC-VISIB	√
UK	4.6612	X	5.8625	5	-6.2967	X	175.6069	X	-0.3988	SLP-PRECP	√
US	3.1326	X	2.7805	2	-6.4451	√	633.7155	X	-0.3499	SLP-PRECP	√
Emerging countries											
Brazil	9.6139	X	1.8246	3	-5.0831	√	164.6434	X	-0.4730	SKC-TEMP	√
China	6.0818	X	7.4451	4	-5.5700	X	139.5591	X	-0.5926	SLP-TEMP	√
Czech Republic	12.0555	X	11.7784	2	-6.1663	X	192.3352	X	0.3481	VISIB-WIND	√
India	10.0431	X	0.2710	2	-5.5170	√	191.7314	X	0.2223	SKC-TEMP	√
Malaysia	4.4723	X	2.1280	3	-6.4513	√	163.1029	X	-0.3774	SLP-TEMP	√
Mexico	4.1388	X	4.5600	2	-5.7275	√	154.5287	X	-0.5505	SLP-TEMP	√
Poland	5.4334	X	1.1162	2	-5.7121	√	129.2422	X	-0.3031	SKC-VISIB	√
Russia	2.8957	X	0.1155	2	-4.6963	√	141.8236	X	0.3529	SLP-VISIB	√
South Africa	3.2362	X	4.2320	3	-6.0402	X	181.2047	X	-0.4991	SKC-TEMP	√
Turkey	3.0278	X	3.4481	2	-4.6727	√	163.8819	X	0.3404	SKC-WIND	√

Table 12: Results of the OLS regression model 1996-2011 with different means of data deseazonalizing. We report the estimates for each explanatory variable and in brackets we show the standard error of the estimators. Significance level: * (10%), ** (5%) and *** (1%). Scaled numbers by 100.

	α	Rt-1	PRECP	SKC	SLP	TEMP	VISIB	WIND	DJAN	DMON
Developed countries										
Australia	0.0361**	-2.2559	-0.0169	-0.0026	0.0003	-0.0031	0.0029	0.0003	-0.0545	0.0213
	(0.0166)	(1.9700)	(0.0500)	(0.0084)	(0.0004)	(0.0105)	(0.0132)	(0.0008)	(0.0498)	(0.0373)
Canada	0.0397**	3.3415*	-0.0637	0.0056	0.0004	0.0031	-0.0001	0.0002	0.0075	-0.0003
	(0.0182)	(2.0149)	(0.0996)	(0.0070)	(0.0079)	(0.0124)	(0.0008)	(0.0004)	(0.0572)	(0.0382)
France	0.0295	2.2102	-0.3932**	-0.0035	-0.0002	-0.0211**	0.0228	-0.0016	0.0005	-0.0094
	(0.0214)	(1.7079)	(0.1581)	(0.0142)	(0.0004)	(0.0097)	(0.0145)	(0.0015)	(0.0686)	(0.0494)
Germany	0.0187	-0.6786	-0.2751	0.0148	0.0001	-0.0017	0.0304	-0.0004	-0.0338	0.0569
	(0.0257)	(1.9518)	(0.1830)	(0.0147)	(0.0005)	(0.0068)	(0.0278)	(0.0019)	(0.0768)	(0.0591)
Italy	0.0267	1.2604	-0.2057***	-0.0227	0.0013**	-0.0375***	0.0436***	-0.0025	0.0479	-0.0500
	(0.02330	(1.5909)	(0.0674)	(0.0141)	(0.0006)	(0.0130)	(0.0162)	(0.0021)	(0.0839)	(0.0538)
Japan	0.0017	2.6117	-0.0090	-0.0176*	0.0003	0.0097	-0.0019	0.0021	-0.0259	-0.0281
	(0.0217)	(1.8650)	(0.0469)	(0.0099)	(0.0005)	(0.0097)	(0.0063)	(0.0017)	(0.0728)	(0.0502)
Netherlands	0.0246	1.3108	0.0963	-0.0066	0.0001	-0.0094	0.0017	-0.0010	-0.0546	0.0569
	(0.0224)	(1.8276)	(0.1404)	(0.0132)	(0.0004)	(0.0110)	(0.0069)	(0.0013)	(0.0678)	(0.0511)
Norway	0.0541**	2.8747	-0.0028	-0.0054	0.0001	-0.0025	0.0071	-0.0027*	-0.0065	-0.0129
	(0.0223)	(2.1027)	(0.0020)	(0.0139)	(0.0003)	(0.0082)	(0.0082)	(0.0016)	(0.0726)	(0.0508)
UK	0.0338*	0.4350	0.1512	0.0033	0.0005	-0.0077	0.0091*	0.0003	-0.0876*	0.0104
	(0.0182)	(1.7789)	(0.1526)	(0.0109)	(0.0003)	(0.0091)	(0.0054)	(0.0013)	(0.0521)	(0.0416)
US	0.0037	-3.3217	0.0750	-0.0107	0.0002	0.0045	0.0010	0.0000	-0.0055	0.0114
	(0.0174)	(2.1255)	(0.0512)	(0.0076)	(0.0003)	(0.0061)	(0.0117)	(0.0009)	(0.0530)	(0.0364)
Emerging countries										
Brazil	0.0925***	3.1613	-0.1733	0.0052	0.0009	-0.0264	0.0371	0.0029	-0.0156	-0.1553**
	(0.0335)	(2.0497)	(0.2086)	(0.0197)	(0.0016)	(0.0198)	(0.0318)	(0.0030)	(0.1157)	(0.0768)
China	0.0189	-0.1491	-0.0409	0.0020	0.0002	-0.0029	-0.0092	0.0017	0.0071	0.1160*
	(0.0249)	(1.5997)	(0.0680)	(0.0109)	(0.0009)	(0.0139)	(0.0108)	(0.0023)	(0.0846)	(0.0622)
Czech Republic	0.0193	5.5212**	0.1237	0.0123	0.0006	-0.0144**	0.0027	0.0001	0.0254	0.0223
	(0.0210)	(2.5207)	(0.1378)	(0.0107)	(0.0004)	(0.0072)	(0.0049)	(0.0018)	(0.0679)	(0.0442)
India	0.0298***	8.6071	-0.0167	-0.0144	0.0033	-0.0069	0.0965*	-0.0027	-0.1078	0.1109*
	(0.0266)	(2.0509)	(0.0325)	(0.0233)	(0.0021)	(0.0237)	(0.0581)	(0.0028)	(0.0886)	(0.0647)
Malaysia	0.0317*	16.4331***	-0.0014	-0.0401	0.0011	0.0201	0.0266	-0.0035	0.0687	-0.1514***
	(0.0170)	(2.1288)	(0.0291)	(0.0577)	(0.0019)	(0.0158)	(0.0193)	(0.0030)	(0.0558)	(0.0380)
Mexico	0.0751***	11.0772***	0.1423	-0.0129	0.0000	0.0032	-0.0117	0.0025	-0.0492	-0.0976**
	(0.0245)	(1.8805)	(0.1081)	(0.0118)	(0.0010)	(0.0129)	(0.0143)	(0.0023)	(0.0810)	(0.0543)
Poland	0.0184	11.7029***	-0.0594	-0.0143	0.0000	0.0080	0.0236	-0.0039**	0.1195	0.0582
	(0.0243)	(1.8844)	(0.1493)	(0.0161)	(0.0005)	(0.0099)	(0.0182)	(0.0017)	(0.0893)	(0.0567)
Russia	0.0566	13.0208***	0.0325	-0.0246	-0.0001	0.0076	0.0091	-0.0008	-0.0415	0.1081
	(0.0414)	(2.0851)	(1.0862)	(0.0213)	(0.0007)	(0.0123)	(0.0082)	(0.0033)	(0.1323)	(0.0907)
South Africa	0.0259	7.7365***	0.0347	-0.0136	0.0002	-0.0075	-0.0173	0.0015	0.0265	0.1254***
	(0.0203)	(1.8164)	(0.0924)	(0.0182)	(0.0002)	(0.0096)	(0.0151)	(0.0018)	(0.0735)	(0.0465)
Turkey	0.1569***	4.3203**	-0.0853	0.0414	0.0197	0.0230	0.1098*	0.0018	0.1053	-0.2873***
	(0.0411)	(2.0308)	(0.1872)	(0.0264)	(0.0122)	(0.0222)	(0.0615)	(0.0026)	(0.1421)	(0.0957)

Taking into consideration the results of table 4 and table 12, we discover a slight change in the coefficients signs. By using the new means of seasonal adjustment we obtain coefficients that are more frequently in agreement with the expectations. On average, the coefficients have the anticipated signs in almost all countries. On the other hand, the Hirshleifer and Schumway (2003) deseasonalizing method causes more erratic patterns of the coefficients signs that are in disagreement with the anticipations. Table 13 presents an overview of the of the significant variables in emerging and developed countries.

Table 13: An overview of the significant weather variables for each country over the period 1996-2011 with a different means of data deseazonalizing. The significance level is set to 10% and less.

Developed		Emerging	
Australia	-	Brazil	-
Canada	-	China	-
France	PRECP, TEMP	Czech Republic	TEMP
Germany	-	India	VISIB
Italy	PRECP, SLP, TEMP, VISIB	Malaysia	-
Japan	SKC	Mexico	-
Netherlands	-	Poland	WIND
Norway	WIND	Russia	-
UK	VISIB	South Africa	-
US	-	Turkey	VISIB

Based on these results, the weather effect is more influential (although almost non-existing) on stock returns than previously concluded. We identify more significant variables and, judging by the size of the coefficients, with comparable impact on stock returns as noted in Section 4. Given these consistent results, we conclude that the weather influence is minimal, at best non-existent. Moreover, there is no difference between emerging and developed countries. Emerging countries do not appear to be present significant weather variables more often than developed countries, although they do seem to be more inefficient based on recurring significance associated with the lagged return and Monday effect.

5.2.   Joint tests

5.2.1   Pooled least squares regression

Table 14 shows the results of pooled regression for the entire time sample. Only visibility (VISIB) is significant over the entire period for the emerging countries; however, the sign is different from what was anticipated. None of the explanatory weather variables are significant for the world and developed countries. Based on these results, it can be concluded that there is no difference regarding the weather effect in emerging and developed countries. In addition, the general conclusion is that the weather effect is not present over the the analized period, given both means of seasonal adjustment.

Table 14: The results of pooled regressions for the period 1996-2011 with a different means of data deseasonalizing. We report the estimates for each explanatory variable and in brackets we show the standard error of the estimators. Significance level: * (10%), ** (5%) and *** (1%). Scaled numbers by 100.

	α	Rt-1	PRECP	SKC	SLP	TEMP	VISIB	WIND	DJAN	DMON
World	0.0405***	5.3573***	-0.0032	-0.0037	0.0001	-0.0020	0.0017	-0.0001	-0.0038	-0.0033
	(0.0145)	(0.8843)	(0.0020)	(0.0031)	(0.0001)	(0.0027)	(0.0027)	(0.0004)	(0.0449)	(0.0353)
Developed countries	0.0296*	0.8152	-0.0029	-0.0045	0.0000	-0.0037	-0.0053	-0.0005	-0.0252	0.0054
	(0.0159)	(1.2528)	(0.0020)	(0.0037)	(0.0002)	(0.0037)	(0.0033)	(0.0005)	(0.0468)	(0.0371)
Emerging countries	0.0518***	7.8202***	-0.0130	-0.0010	0.0003	0.0017	-0.0073*	0.0004	0.0151	-0.0131
	(0.0154)	(0.9456)	(0.0210)	(0.0055)	(0.0002)	(0.0042)	(0.0041)	(0.0008)	(0.0508)	(0.0382)

In order to check for a weather effect pattern, we run regressions by forming similar subsamples as in Section 4. Results in table 15 and 16 show that both developed countries and emerging countries display that the weather effect is only significant for the periods 1996-1998 and 1999-2001. Thereafter, none of the weather variables is significant. This might explain the non-appearance of the weather effect during the entire period (world analysis). Based on these results, we infer that the weather effect vanishes over time.

During the first two periods cloud coverage (SKC), temperature (TEMP) and visibility (VISIB) are the most important weather variables (see table 16). The least significant variables are precipitation (PRECP), sea level pressure (SLP) and wind speed (WIND). With respect to the accuracy of the signs, there are only a few numbers of variables that do not comply with the expectations.

Table 15: Significant weather variables for the world (20 countries), the developed countries and the emerging countries for different periods in time within the total period 1996-2011 with a different means of data deseasonalizing. OLS regression model is used with non-overlapping data. Weather variables confidence level is set to 90%.

	World	Developed countries	Emerging countries
1996-1998	SKC	SKC,VISIB	SKC
1999-2001	SLP,TEMP,WIND	TEMP	TEMP,VISIB
2002-2004	-	-	-
2005-2007	-	-	-
2008-2011	-	-	-

Table 16: Significant weather variables for the world (20 countries), the developed countries and the emerging countries for rolling 3 year periods with a different means of data deseasonalizing. OLS regression model. Weather variables confidence level is set to 90%.

	World	Developed countries	Emerging countries
1996-1998	SKC	SKC,VISIB	SKC
1997-1999	SKC	SKC,SLP,VISIB	-
1998-2000	PRECP,TEMP	SKC	TEMP
1999-2001	SLP,TEMP,WIND	TEMP	TEMP,VISIB
2000-2002	SLP	-	SKC
2001-2003	-	-	-
2002-2004	-	-	-
2003-2005	-	-	-
2004-2006	-	-	-
2005-2007	-	-	-
2006-2008	-	-	-
2007-2009	-	SKC	-
2008-2010	-	-	-
2009-2011	-	-	SLP

It can be infered that the year when the weather effect loses significance is different for developed and emerging countries. For the developed countries, the least significant period for the weather effect is between 2001 and 2007, while for the emerging countries the least significant period for the weather effect is between 2002 and 2009. These findings are largely consistent with the results of non-overlapping data.

Nonetheless, the conclusion we draw from the results of this section only partly corresponds with the Section 4 inference. By using the Hirshleifer and Schumway (2003) deseasonalizing method the weather variables are starting to lose significance after the year of 2001, which corresponds with de-creasing pattern of the weather variables identified in this section. However, we find little support of a cyclical pattern of the weather effect.

5.2.2. Binary regression

The results of binary regressions are shown table 17, while table 18 presents the marginal effects of weather on stock returns. Only developed countries appear to bear a influence of weather over stock returns. However, given the very small coefficients and the small number of significant variables, we cannot assume a systematic difference between emerging and developed countries. These results sup-port the findings of Section 4 concluding that there is no difference between developed and emerging countries in terms of the weather effect, while judging by the size of the coefficients the weather does have a larger influence on the magnitude of returns compared to their level.

Table 17: Logit estimation of the probability of having a positive stock return over the period 1996-2011 for the world (20 countries), developed countries and emerging countries with a different means of data deseasonalizing. Standard errors are reported between parentheses. Significance level: * (10%), ** (5%) and *** (1%).

	α	PRECP	SKC	SLP	TEMP	VISIB	WIND
World	0.2049***	-0.0025	-0.0085**	0.0001	-0.0017	0.0008	-0.0008
	(0.0070)	(0.0035)	(0.0043)	(0.0002)	(0.0030)	(0.0033)	(0.0005)
Developed countries	0.1949***	-0.0025	-0.0079	0.0000	-0.0050	0.0101**	-0.0013*
	(0.0098)	(0.0035)	(0.0056)	(0.0002)	(0.0040)	(0.0051)	(0.0007)
Emerging countries	0.2149***	-0.0071	-0.0071	0.0004	0.0045	-0.0063	0.0000
	(0.0098)	(0.0327)	(0.0066)	(0.0003)	(0.0050)	(0.0044)	(0.0009)

Table 18: Marginal effects for probability of an upward stock market by using the logit model, for the world (20 countries), developed countries and emerging countries with a different means of data deseasonalizing.

	α	PRECP	SKC	SLP	TEMP	VISIB	WIND
World	0.1129	-0.0014	-0.0047	0.0001	-0.0010	0.0004	-0.0004
Developed countries	0.1069	-0.0014	-0.0043	0.0000	-0.0027	0.0055	-0.0007
Emerging countries	0.1190	-0.0039	-0.0039	0.0002	0.0025	-0.0035	0.0000

Moreover, the corresponding signs are on average correct. In the world regression, only cloud cover is found significant. A 1 unit increase in the excess cloud coverage (SKC) around the world will cause a decrease in the probability that the stock market returns are positive with 0.0047 percetange points. A 1 unit increase in visibility (VISIB) and wind speed (WIND) will increase, respectively decrease, the probability that the market returns are positive with 0.0055 and 0.0007 percentage points for the developed countries.

6. Potential explanations

The results of previous sections guide us to the conclusion that the weather effect has minimal impact on stock returns; at best there is no weather influence at all. This is supported by both Section 4 and Section 5 where different deseasonalizing methods are used. Furthermore, the results of previous sections guide us to the conclusion that there is no significant difference between emerging and developed markets in terms of weather effect. This has never been investigated by other authors, but the conclusion is supported by mixed results on individual countries analyses that suggest no systematic distinction between emerging and developed countries. The results hold even after performing robustness check tests.

In addition to this, we identify that the weather effect has a cyclical pattern over time. Weather appears to be significant in times that largely correspond to expansion and highly speculative periods, whereas no significant weather variable is found for periods that overlap crisis periods. A potential rationalization that would justify this result lies in irrational exuberance. When stock markets are driven by irrational bubbles, then more anomalies emerge on the markets and irrational investors take over. In expansion times stock prices might be overvalued due to a large number of irrational investors. They drive stock prices in a manner that is less according to fundamental values and more base on noise trade and psychology. Thus, they might be more influenced by weather. However, when the bubble bursts and in periods of crisis, the markets suffer corrections and irrational behavior is drastically reduced. Crisis clears the markets and allow for less deviations from fundamentals. Hence, irrational investors - that might be to a certain extent influenced by weather, disappear.

Nonetheless, this finding does not hold when confronted with the second deseasonalizing method. This might be due to the fact that this means of seasonal adjustment is harsher on the excess variables and cuts a part of weather effects. By computing an average for each week based on the entire sample, excess variables are larger than when a weekly average is subtracted. This might artificially favor relationship between weather and stock returns. Also, by comparing the two methods of seasonal adjustment based on the number of correctly resulting coefficients signs, the second method is superior. On average, it has an accuracy of over 75%, whereas the Hirshleifer and Schumway (2003) method only determines approximately 50% of the anticipated common-sense signs.

In addition, the weather influence fades in time during the 1996-2011 period. This is supported by the loss in the significance level for the first means of seasonal adjustment and the lack of significant weather variables for the second means. Previous literature provides support for this statement. Saunders (1993) noticed that the weather effect is more influential within the period 1982-1989 was much than the period before it (starting in 1962). Further, Akhtari (2011) studied the period 1948-2010 for the US and noticed that the weather effect is stronger in some periods, while it ceases during others. He finds that weather has more impact during 1990-1997. According to his study, weather has a cyclical effect. Hirshleifer and Schumway (2003) studied 26 countries over the period 1982-1997 and found significant weather effect. As can be inferred from prior studies, the weather effect is time-dependent.

Our results indicate that the weather effect was more influential in terms of the magnitude of the coefficients and significance level before 2001 for developed countries and around 2002 for emerging countries. Also, overall data indicates that 2001 is a cut-off date. These different break-points can be assimilated together as emerging countries usually follow the trend of developed ones, but present some delays in terms of events reaction. A potential explanation for the delayed breaking point of emerging countries is that there is a time lag between the developments in the emerging markets and the developments originated in the developed markets. Dooley and Hutchison (2009) reached a similar conclusion in their study that focused on the financial crisis starting in 2007. The stock markets of emerging countries seemed to be decoupled for some months (early 2007 to summer 2008) from the developments on the financial market of the United States. Thereafter, the emerging markets and the United States market were highly related.

Hence, based on the rolling window panel data regressions and generally acceptance of emerging stock markets delays compared to developed markets, we set the year 2001 as a cut-off point for our data. Starting from 1996 to 2001 weather is a significant determinant of stock returns, whereas from 2001 to 2011 the weather effect vanishes. The main methodology, however, only partly supports 2001 as a cut-off values. Results in Section 4 do show a drop in the significance of the weather variables, but the the number of significant variables varies in time in a cyclical manner. Nevertheless, both the main methodology and the robustness check indicate 2001 as a significant year in terms of how the weather effect appears. Despite the fact that only the second means of data deseasonalizing shows a clear diminishing pattern of the weather effect, the aforementioned year appears to be significant in the main methodology as well.

This break-year seems to be related to the Internet bubble. During the Internet boom investing became popular and it became a social happening. Moreover, the number of social investments clubs was increasing during this period. Noteworthy, there was a sharp boost in the number of individual investors, often regarded as irrational noisy traders and more susceptible to inducing mispricing errors than institutional investors. Therefore, individual investors are more likely to be affected by social influences, psychology and weather. This can partly explain the significant weather effect before 2001. The peak of this speculative bubble was in March 2000. When the Internet bubble burst, individual investors lost their savings and value of assets and flee the stock market, reluctant to continue investing. Their stock market activity became less frequent after this speculative bubble burst (and it might have taken some months until markets were noise trader free) and markets were dominated by rational investors. Along with the diminishing number of individual investors, the mood and weather effect lost significance.

Furthermore, Shiller (1984) noticed that between 1970 and 1980 the numbers of irrational investors was increasing in the US. This observation coincides with weather effect studies that use the same time span and conclude that weather is influential upon stock returns in the US (Akhtari, 2011; Saunders, 1993). We can thus infer that the decreasing weather effect is based on the reduction of the number of irrational investors that activate on the market.

Another argument that supports that the Internet bubble has been a turning point for stock markets is related to investors' psychology. Not only did this speculative bubble cause a structural change on the stock markets, but it also had a significant impact on investor behavior. The significant price deviation from economic efficiency during the late 1990s that cannot be explained by economic fundamentals such as the cost of capital, inflation, GDP growth can only be attributed to investors' psychology. In the aftermath of the bubble burst, investors changed their means of forming expectations, while over-confidence and anchoring became less relevant as a behavioral manifestation.

Whale and Amin (2010) explore the psychology of investors during the pre and post market capitula-tion in the spring of 2000. They focus their study on heuristic-driven bias and frame dependence and provide evidence that these market anomalies have become less pronounced after the Internet bubble burst. They find that heuristic-driven decisions – that entail choices without complete assessment of the situations, are more frequent before the Dotcom bubble and reflect that investors' predictions are too far from the mean performance of the actual companies. Also, overconfidence such as frame de-pendence – when investors are highly selective of available data and cultivate a high risk tolerance, has changed after the speculative bubble burst. Hence, stock markets have exhibited less behavioral influence after the burst of the Internet bubble, respectively after the year 2000.

In addition to this, we based our expectations regarding a more prominent weather effect in emerging countries compared to developed ones on the assumption that the former are less efficient. However, there are studies that support that emerging stock markets are progressing in terms of efficiency and slowly converging to developed markets traits. Griffin, Kelly and Nardaric (2009) found over the peri-od 1994-2005 that emerging stock markets are very similar to developed stock markets in terms of efficiency. Further, our emerging markets dataset is based on criteria that classify the countries as ad-vanced emerging. This implies that the difference between developed and emerging countries is not remarkably large. Nonetheless, secondary emerging countries have discontinuous and erratic trading patterns that would negatively influence the quality of our data.

The paper provides no support for a significant difference in the weather effect between developed and emerging countries. This can be be explained the convergence process that has accelerated over the last 30 years. This implies that emerging countries grow at faster rates than developed countries while replicating the methods, technologies, processes and institutions of developed countries. Waheeduz-zaman (2011) found support for the convergence between emerging and developed markets. The big-gest emerging markets showed a higher growth in GDP, investments and trade compared to the G7 countries over a 30-year period between 1980 and 2010. The G7 countries, however, still have a sub-stantial lead. Based on their results, we infer that investments and trade characteristics of emerging and developed countries are becoming more and more similar over time.

7. Conclusion

This study has examined if weather has a significant influence on stock returns. The central aim of this paper is to make a distinction between emerging and developed countries and to investigate if the weather effect has a different impact depending on the stock market development. Also, we refine our research question by analyzing if the weather effect has changed over time in both emerging and developed countries. In order to check for robust results, two methods of data deseasonalizing are employed.

The approach used in this paper in order to research the weather effect focuses on six weather variables: precipitation, sea level pressure, sky cloud cover, air temperature, visibility and wind speed rate. We conduct multivariate regressions on individual countries, then on the aggregate emerging and developed countries, followed by a logit model that model the probability of recording positive returns. This study spans over 16 years between 1996 and 2011 and entails 10 developed and 10 emerging countries. In order to examine the changes in the weather effect over time, 3 year subsamples of both overlapping and non-overlapping data are employed.

This paper contributes to prior literature by making a clear distinction between emerging and developed countries. Although the weather variables we use have been individually analyzed by other authors, they have never been used altogether in a multivariate regression. The time analysis is also a novel addition that captures investors' behavior and weather influence during different stages of economic cycle. We also account for most of the critical points that have been brought upon Hirshleifer and Schumway (2003) concerning coincidental macroeconomic events, the timing of the sample and weather variable collection. Also, we provide an innovative means of data deseazonalizing so as to account for potential look-ahead biases and global warming (highly significant according to NASA data, see figure 3).

The results of this study indicate that the presence of the weather effect is modest and almost non-existing in both emerging and developed countries. There is no systematic difference regarding the impact of weather based on stock market characteristics. Hence, it is nearly impossible to build a trading strategy based on weather features, especially if we were to consider the amount of transaction cost that would accrue as a result of daily trading due to changing weather, not to mention weather conditions unpredictability. Moreover, the weather effect appears to be more significant within the period 1996-2001 and weakens after 2001 in both emerging and developed countries. Also, emerging countries tend to be more inefficient compared to developed ones. We also show that the magnitude of stock returns is influenced more by the weather variables compared to stock returns level.

Although some weather variables appear to be significant in some countries, their impact is so small that we cannot infer that weather has explanatory power over stock returns. Emerging and developed countries show no different patterns in terms of weather effect. This can be attributed mainly to emerging stock markets increasing efficiency over the last 20 years – although they have not reached the same level of efficiency as developed states, and the convergence process that has propelled developing countries towards a more competitive stock market infrastructure.

The results of this study identify 2001 as a breaking point within our sample. The weather effect tends to have a recurring pattern; nonetheless, the intensity of the weather influence decreases after 2001. This can be related to the burst of the Internet bubble and further changes that it induced on the stock markets. First, the number of household investors has peaked in the year 2000 and has not grew as much in following exuberance periods. Secondly, this structural adjustment is reinforced by investors' behavior change.

Further research includes investigating the effect of weather on stock market volatility and trading behavior. Even though stock returns are only moderately influenced by weather, erratic and extreme weather conditions might have more impact on stock returns volatility. Also, weather affects investors' mood and this might be reflected by their subsequent behavior and trading patterns within the day such as the trading volume or the number of transactions. Weather-induced optimism might boost the trading volume due to an increased risk-taking attitude.

Also, some of the assumptions we have made can be extended. For instance, our motivation towards this research was that emerging countries are more segmented and the number of individual and domestic investors is higher than compared to developed countries. We presume that these are more influenced by local weather conditions than other types of investors, hence we expected emerging countries to display a larger weather effect than developed countries. However, our findings show that there is no difference regarding the weather effect. This result provides further incentive so as to research if weather has a distinct impact on stock returns while making distinctions between agent types. Additional data would be needed on the number of individual accounts, the proportion of institutional investors, the proportion of domestic investors as compared to foreign investors etc.

8. References

Akhtari, M. (2011). Reassessment of the Weather Effect: Stock Prices and Wall Street Weather. *Undergraduate Economic Review*, 7 (1), 1-25.

Allen, A.M. and Fisher, G.J. (1978). Ambient Temperature Effects on Paired Associate Learning. *Ergonomics,* 21 (2), 95-101.

Anderson, C.A. (2001). Heat and Violence. *Current Directions in Psychological Science*, 10 (1), 33-38.

Arkes, H.R., Herren, L.T. and Isen, A.M. (1988). The Role of Potential Loss in the Influence of Affect on Risk-taking Behavior. *Organizational Behavior and Human Decision Process,* 42 (2), 181-193.

Au, K., Chan, F., Wang, D. and Vertinsky, I. (2003). Mood in Foreign Exchange Trading: Cognitive Processes and Performance. *Organizational Behavior and Human Decision Processes*, 91 (2), 322-338.

Bagozzi, R., Gopinath, M. and Nyer, P. (1999). The Role of Emotions in Marketing. *Journal of Academy of Marketing Science,* 27 (2), 184-206.

Barberis, N. and Thaler, R. (2002). A Survey of Behavioral Finance. *National Bureau of Economic Research*. Working Paper 9222, 1051-1121.

Bekaert, G. and Harvey C.R. (1998). Capital Markets: An Engine for Economic Growth. *Brown Journal of World Affairs*. 5(1), 33-53.

Bell, P.A. and Baron, R.A. (1976). Aggression and Heat: The Mediating Role of Negative Affect. *Journal of Applied Social Psychology*, 6 (1), 18-30.

Brooks, C.(2008). *Introductory Econometrics for Finance*. Cambridge. Cambridge University Press.

Brown, G.W. (1999). Volatility, Sentiment, and Noise Traders. *Financial Analysts Journal*, 55 (2), 82-90.

Cao, M. and Wei, J. (2005). Stock Market Returns: A Note on Temperature Anomaly. *Journal of Banking and Finance*, 29 (6), 1559–1573.

Chang, S.C., Chen, S.S., Chou, R. and Lin, Y.H. (2008). Weather and Intraday Patterns in Stock Returns and Trading Activity. *Journal of Banking and Finance*, 32 (9), 1754-1766.

Chang, T., Nieh, C.C., Yang, M.J. and Yang, T.Y. (2006). Are Stock Market Returns related to the Weather Effects? Empirical Evidence from Taiwan. *Physica A*, 364, 343-354.

Conlisk, J. (1996). Why Bounded Rationality?. *Journal of Economic Literature*, 34 (2), 669-700.

Cunningham, M.R. (1979). Weather, Mood and helping Behavior: Quasi- Experiment with the Sunshine Samaritan. *Journal of Personality and Social Psychology,* 37 (11), 1947-1956.

Denissen, J.J.A., Penke, L., Butalid, L. and Van Aken, M.A.G. (2008). The Effects of Weather on Daily Mood: A Multilevel Approach. *Emotion,* 8 (5), 662-667.

Digon, E. and Bock, H. (1966). Suicides and Climatology. *Archives of Environmental Health*, 12, 279-

286.

Dooley, M. and Hutchison, M. (2009). Transmission of the U.S. Subprime Crisis to Emerging
Markets: Evidence on the Decoupling–recoupling Hypothesis. *Journal of International Money
and Finance*, 28, 1331-1349.

Dowling, M. and Lucey, B. (2005). Weather, Biorhythms, Beliefs and Stock Returns - Some
preliminary Irish Evidence. *International Review of Financial Analysis,* 14 (3), 337-355.

Fama, E.F. (1970). Efficient Capital Markets: A Review of Theory and Empirical Work. *The Journal
of Finance*, 25 (2), 383-417.

Floros, F. (2011). On the Relationship between Weather and Stock Market Returns. *Studies in
Economics and Finance*, 28 (1), 5-13.

Forgas, J.P. (2005). Mood and Judgment: The Affect Infusion Model (AIM). *Psychological Bulletin*,
117 (1), 39-66.

Gerlach, J.F. (2007). Macroeconomic News and Stock Market Calendar and Weather Anomalies.
The Journal of Financial Research, 30 (2), 283-300.

Goetzmann, W.N. and Zhu, N. (2003). Rain or Shine: Where is the Weather Effect?. *National Bureau
of Economic Research*. Working Paper 9465, 1-29.

Griffin, J.M, Kelly, P.J., Nardaric, F., (2009). Are Emerging Markets More Profitable? Implications
for Comparing Weak and Semi-Strong Form Efficiency. *Social Science Research Network*,
working   paper number 959006.

Gujarati, D.N. (2004). *Basic Econometrics*. New York. McGraw Hill.

Hampel, F.R., Ronchetti, E.M., Rousseeuw, P.J., Stahel, W.A. (2011). *Robust Statistics – the
Approach Based on Influence Factors*. John Wiley & Sons.

Harvey, C. R. (1994). Predictable Risk and Returns in Emerging Markets. *National Bureau of
Economic Research*. Working Paper 4621, 1-57.

Haugen, R.A., Philippe, J. (1996) The January effect: Still there after all these years. *Financial
Analysts Journal,* 52(1) 27-31.

Hirshleifer, D. and Shumway, T. (2003). Good Day Sunshine: Stock Returns and the Weather.
The Journal of Finance, 58 (3), 1009-1032.

Howarth, E. and Hoffman, M.S. (1984). A Multidimensional Approach to the Relationship between
Mood and Weather. *British Journal of Psychology*, 75, 15-23.

Jaffe, J., Westerfield, R. (1985). The Week-End Effect in Common Stock Returns: The International
Evidence. *The Journal of Finance*, 40 (2), 433-454.

Jacobsen, B. and Marquering, W. (2008). Is it the Weather? *Journal of Banking and Finance,* 32, 526-
540.

Johnson, E.J. and Tversky, A. (1983). Affect, Generalization and the Perception of Risk. *Journal of
Personality and Social Psychology*, 45 (1), 20-31.

Kals, W.S. (1982). *Your Health, your Moods and the Weather (*1st edition). New York: Doubleday.

Kamara, A. New Evidence on the Monday Seasonal in Stock Returns. *The Journal of Business*, 70 (1), 63-84.

Kamstra, M.J., Kramer, L.A. and Levi, M.D. (2003). Winter Blues: A SAD Stock Market Cycle. *American Economic Review*, 93 (1), 324-333.

Kang, S.H., Jiang, Z., Lee, Y. and Yoon, S.M. (2010). Weather effects on the returns and volatility of the Shanghai stock market. *Physica A*, 389, 91-99.

Kaustia, M. and Rantapuska, E. (2011). Does mood affect trading behavior?. SSRN, working paper series 1875645, 1-44.

Keef, S.P. and Roush M.L. (2002). The Weather and Stock Returns in New Zealand. *Quarterly Journal of Business and Economics*, 41 (1 and 2), 61-79.Korajczyk, R. A. (1996). A Measure of Stock Market Integration for Developed and Emerging Markets. *The World Bank Economic Review*. 10 (2), 267-289.

Krämer, W. and Runde, R. (1997) Stock and Weather: An Exercise in Data Mining or yet another Capital Market Anomaly?. *Empirical Economics*. 22, 637-641.

Kuhnen, C.A. and Knutson, B. (2011). The Influence of Affect on Beliefs, Preferences and Financial Decisions. *Journal of Financial and Quantitative Analysis*, 46 (3), 605-626.

Lakonishok, J., Smidt, S. (1988) Are Seasonal Anomalies Real? A Ninety-Year Perspective. *The Review of Financial Studies*, 1 (4), 403-425.

Lee, Y.M. and Wang, K.M. (2011). The Effectiveness of the Sunshine Effect in Taiwan's stock market before and after the 1997 financial crisis. *Economic Modelling*, 28, 710-727.

Levy, O. and Galili, I. (2008). Stock Purchase and the Weather: Individual Differences. *Journal of Economic Behavior and Organization*, 67, 755-767.

Loewenstein, G.F. (2000). Emotions in Economic Theory and Economic Behavior. *The American Economic Review*, 90 (2), 426-432.

Loewenstein, G.F., Elke, U.W., Christopher, K.H. and Welch N. (2001). Risk as Feelings. *Psychological Bulletin*, 127 (2), 267-286.

Loughran, T. and Schultz, P. (2004). Weather, Stock Returns, and the Impact of Localized Trading Behavior. *Journal of Financial and Quantitative Analysis*, 39 (2), 343-364.

Lu, J. and Chou, R.K. (2012). Does the Weather have impacts on Returns and Trading Activities in Order-Driven Stock Markets? Evidence from China. *Journal of Empirical Finance*, 19, 79–93.

Mehra, R. and Sah, R.(2002). Mood Fluctuations, Projection Bias, and Volatility of Equity Prices. *Journal of Economics Dynamics and Control*, 26, 869-887.

Newey, W.K, West, K.D. (1987). A Simple Positive-Definite Heteroskedasticity and Autocorrelation-Consistent Covariance Matrix. *Econometrica*. 55, 703-708.

Page, L., Hajat, S. and Kovats, R. (2007). Relationship between Daily Suicide Counts and Temperature in England and Wales. *British Journal of Psychiatry*, 191, 106-112.

Pardo, A. and Valor, E. (2003). Spanish Stock Returns: Where is the Weather Effect?. *European Financial Management*, 9 (1), 117-126

Saunders, E.M. Jr. (1993). Stock Prices and Wall Street Weather. *The American Economic Review*, 83 (5), 1337-1345.

Schneider, F.W., Lesko, W.A. and Garrett, W.A. (1980). Helping Behavior in Hot, Comfortable and Cold Temperature: A Field Study. *Environment and Behavior*, 12 (2), 231-241.

Schwarz, N. and Clore, G.L. (1983). Mood, Misattribution, and Judgments of Well-being: Informative and Directive Functions of Affective States. *Journal of Personality and Social Psychology*, 45 (3), 513-523.

Shalen, C. (1993). Volume, Volatility, and the Dispersion of Beliefs. *Review of Financial Studies*, 6 (2), 405-434.

Shiller, R.J. (2003). From Efficient Markets Theory to Behavioral Finance. *The Journal of Economic Perspectives*, 17 (1), 83-104.

Shu, H.C. (2008). Weather, Investor Sentiment and Stock Market Returns: Evidence from Taiwan. *The Journal of American Academy of Business*, 14 (1), 96-102.

Simon, H.A. (1955). A behavioral model of rational choice. *The Quarterly Journal of Economics*, 69 (1), 99-118.

Sriboonchitta, S., Chitip, P., Sriwichailampham, T. and Chaiboonsri, C. (2011). Stock Market Returns and the Temperature Effect: Thailand. *International Research Journal of Management and Business Studies*, 1 (1), 12-16.

Symeonidis, L., Daskalakis, G. and Markellos, R. (2010). Does the Weather affect Stock Market Volatility?. *Finance Research Letters*, 7, 214-223.

Trombley, M.A. (1997). Stock Price and Wall Street Weather: Additional Evidence. *Quarterly Journal of Business and Economics*, 36, 11-21.

Tufan, E. and Hamarat, B. (2004). Do Cloudy Days Affect Stock Exchange Returns: Evidence from Istanbul Stock Exchange. *Journal of Naval Science and Engineering*, 2 (1), 117-126.

Waheeduzzaman, A.N.M. (2011). Competitiveness and Convergence in G7 and Emerging Markets. *Competitiveness Review: An International Business Journal*, 21 (2), 110-128.

Watson, D. (2000). *Situational and Environmental influence on Mood. In: Mood and Temperament.* New York: Guilford Press.

Wheale, P.R., Amin, L.H. (2010). Bursting the Dotcom Bubble: A Case Study in Investor behavior. *Technology Analysis and Strategic Management.* 15:1, 117-136.

Worthington, A.C. (2006). Whether the Weather: A Comprehensive Assessment of Climate Effects in the Australian Stock Market. *University of Wollongong, School of Accounting and Finance,* Working Paper Series No. 06/17, 1-20.

Wyndham, H.C. (1969). Adaptation to Heat and Cold. *Environmental Research*, 2 (5 and 6), 442-469.

Yoon, S.M. and Kang, S.H. (2009). Weather Effects on Returns: Evidence from the Korean stock
Market. *Physica A*, 388, 682-690.

Yuen, K. S. L. and Lee, T. M. C. (2003). Could Mood State affect Risk-taking Decisions?. *Journal of
Affective Disorders*, 75, 11-18.

Yuksel, A. and Yuksel, A. (2009). Stock Return Seasonality and the Temperature Effect. *International
Research Journal of Finance and Economics*, 34, 107-116.

Yule, G.U. (1974). Why Do We Sometimes Get Nonsense Correlations Between Time Series? A study
in Sampling and the Nature of Time Series. *Journal of the Royal Statistical Society*. 89, 1-64.

9. Appendix

Table 19: Overview of the literature about the relationship between weather variables and the stock market with
the location and time period

Author(s)	Dependent variable(s)	Independent variable(s)	Location	Time period
Akhtari (2011)	Returns, DJIA	Cloud cover (sunshine)	New York City	1948-2010
Cao and Wei (2005)	Returns, 9 international indices	Temperature	US, Canada, Japan, Taiwan, UK, Germany, Sweden, Australia	1994-2004
Chang, Chen, Chou and Li (2008)	Returns (NYSE), trading activity (volume, bid-ask spread, quoted depth, volatility and order imbalance)	Rain, cloud cover, temperature, snow, wind speed	New York City	1994-2004
Chang, Nieh, Yang and Yang (2006)	Returns, Taiwan stock market	Temperature, humidity, cloud cover	Taiwan	1997-2003
Dowling and Lucey (2005)	Returns, Irish Stock Exchange Official Price Index	Cloud cover, humidity, rain, Geomagnetic storms, SAD, daylight savings time change, lunar phases, Friday thirteenth	Ireland	1988-2001
Floros (2011)	Returns, Portuguese PSI20 index	Temperature	Portugal	1995-2007
Gerlach (2007)	Returns, S&P 500 and equally weighted NYSE/AMEX/NASDAQ	Turn-of-the-month, fall, lunar, rainfall, temperature, January	US	1980-2003
Goetzmann and Zhu (2003)	Returns, NYSE	Cloud cover (sunshine)	US (New York, Los Angeles, San Francisco, Chicago and Philadelphia)	1980-2003
Hirshleifer and Shumway (2003)	Returns, 26 global indices, mostly the capital city	Cloud cover, snow and rain	Global (26 countries)	1982-1997
Jacobsen and Marquering (2008).	Returns, 48 global indices	Temperature, SAD and Halloween	Global (48 countries)	1970-2004
Kamstra, Kramer and Levi (2003)	Returns, 12 indices in total, 4 in US.	SAD, Cloud cover, precipitation, temperature	Global (9 countries)	1928-2001
Kang, Jiang, Lee and Yoon (2010)	Returns and volatility, daily indices Shanghai A-shares and B-shares	Temperature, humidity, sunshine duration	Shanghai	1996-2007
Kaustia and Rantapuska (2011)	Returns and volatility, Helsinki Exchanges,	SAD, daylight, length of the day, lunar phase, precipitation,	Finland	1995-2002

	HEX, nowadays a part of NASDAQ-OMX).	temperature, sunshine		
Keef and Roush (2002)	Returns, value weighted The New Zealand Stock Exchange (NZSE)	Cloud cover, temperature and wind	New Zealand	1986-2002
Krämer and Runde (1997)	Returns, German stock index DAX	Humidity, atmospheric pressure, cloud cover, rain	Germany	1960-1990
Lee and Wang (2011)	Returns, TAIEX index	Cloud cover	Taiwan	1986-2007
Levy and Galili (2008)	Returns, 3283 individual investor accounts of a bank	Cloud cover	Israel	1998-2002
Loughran and Schultz (2004)	Returns, NASDAQ local companies	Cloud cover	US (25 cities)	1984-1997
Lu and Chou (2012)	Returns, Shanghai Stock Exchange	Cloud cover, temperature, humidity, precipitation, visibility	Shanghai	2003-2008
Pardo and Valor (2003)	Returns, Madrid Stock Exchange Index (MSEI)	Sunshine and humidity	Spain, Madrid	1981-2000
Saunders (1993)	Returns, Dow Jones Industrial average and equally and weighted NYSE/AMEX	Cloud cover	New York city	1927-1999
Shu (2008)	Returns and sentiment, Taiwan stock exchange	Temperature, humidity and barometric pressure, (proxy for sunshine)	Taiwan	1995-2004
Sriboonchitta, Chitip, Sriwichailampham and Chaiboonsri (2011)	Returns, Thailand stock exchange	Temperature	Thailand	1996-2010
Trombley (1997)	Returns, DJIA and equally and value weighted CRSP.	Cloud cover	New York City	1927-1992
Tufan and Hamarat (2004)	Returns, Istanbul Stock Exchange	Cloud cover	Istanbul, Turkey	1987-2002
Worthington (2006)	Returns, Australian Stock Exchange (ASX)	Precipitation, humidity, temperature, evaporation, hours sunshine, wind speed	Australia	1958-2005
Yoon and Kang (2009)	Returns, Korea Composite Stock Price Index 200 (KOSPI 200)	Temperature, humidity and cloud cover	Korea	1990-2006
Yuksel and Yuksel (2009)	Returns	Temperature	Global (42 countries)	1997-2008

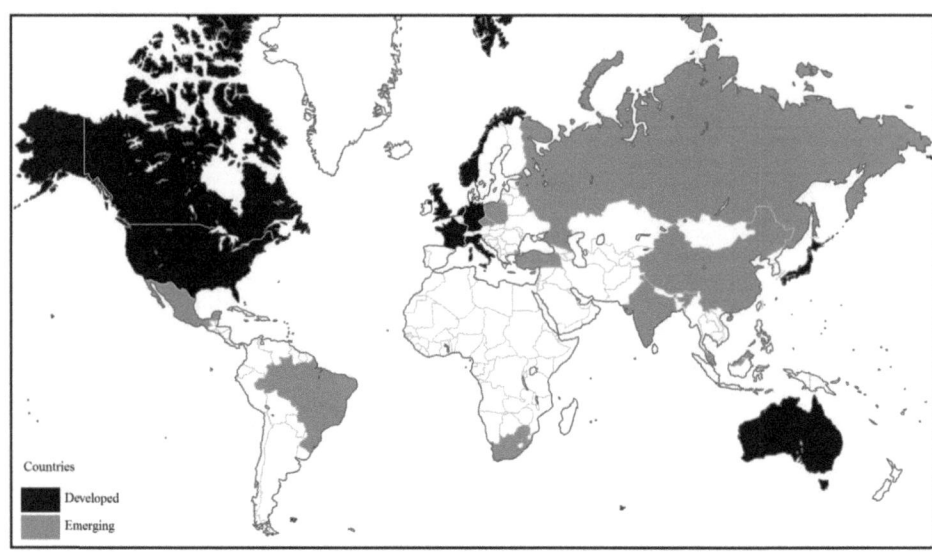

Figure 2:Map of the world including the developed and emerging countries taken into account

Table 20: Overview of the countries with the index and the city that is used. We used data of the weather station that is nearest and has best available data for the weather variables. The indices are retrieved from Datastream.

Country	City	Index	Station: USAF	Station: WBAN
Developed Countries				
Australia	Sydney	FTSE Australia	947670	99999
Canada	Toronto	TSX Composite	712650	99999
France	Paris	CAC All	071570	99999
Germany	Frankfurt	DAX	106330	99999
Italy	Milano	FTSE Italy	160800	99999
Japan	Tokyo	TOPIX	476620	99999
Netherlands	Amsterdam	Amsterdam SE all shares	062400	99999
Norway	Oslo	Oslo exchange all shares	013840	99999
United Kingdom	London	FTSE All share	037720	99999
United States	New York	S&P 500	725030	14732
Emerging countries				
Brazil	Sao Paulo	Bovespa	837800	99999
China	Shanghai	Shanghai SE composite	583670	99999
Czech Republic	Prague	Prague stock exchange	115200	99999
India	Mumbai	BSE 100	430030	99999
Malaysia	Kuala Lumpur	FTSE Bursa Malaysia	468470	99999
Mexico	Mexico City	IPC Bolsa	766800	99999
Poland	Warschau	Warsaw general index	123750	99999
Russia	Moscow	RTS	274790	99999
South Africa	Johannessburg	JSE all share	683680	99999
Turkey	Instanbul	Istanbul SE 100	170600	99999

Table 21: reports the mean, median, standard deviation, kurtosis, skewness, minimum and maximum of the daily raw precipitation (PRECP) over the period 1996-2011. PRECP is the rain and/or melted snow during the day in inches and hundredths. It has a value of at least 0.

	Mean	Median	Standard Deviation	Kurtosis	Skewness	Minimum	Maximum
Developed Countries							
Australia	0.0967	0.0000	0.3271	61.2071	6.7697	0.0000	4.6900
Canada	0.0711	0.0000	0.1872	25.6360	4.4547	0.0000	2.3000
France	0.0674	0.0000	0.1536	24.0037	4.1491	0.0000	1.7100
Germany	0.0533	0.0000	0.1667	148.2148	8.8699	0.0000	4.2500
Italy	0.0773	0.0000	0.3015	284.0839	12.5756	0.0000	9.1300
Japan	0.1691	0.0000	0.4851	44.1153	5.5538	0.0000	6.9700
Netherlands	0.0923	0.0100	0.1862	19.7779	3.7290	0.0000	2.0800
Norway	0.0972	0.0000	0.2376	167.7267	8.3858	0.0000	6.7700
United Kingdom	0.0661	0.0000	0.1389	18.5911	3.6551	0.0000	1.5800
United States	0.1341	0.0000	0.3635	48.2712	5.4777	0.0000	6.4000
Average	0.0925	0.0010	0.2547	84.1628	6.3620		
Emerging countries							
Brazil	0.0870	0.0000	0.2300	39.3427	4.7397	0.0000	4.2200
China	0.1247	0.0000	0.3642	42.7493	5.4737	0.0000	5.4800
Czech Republic	0.0526	0.0000	0.1448	68.3581	6.6034	0.0000	2.4700
India	0.2608	0.0000	0.9168	70.7324	6.7563	0.0000	18.1000
Malaysia	0.2829	0.0200	0.6020	74.0569	5.4219	0.0000	14.0000
Mexico	0.0873	0.0000	0.2304	39.1341	4.7307	0.0000	4.2200
Poland	0.0627	0.0000	0.1692	158.5290	8.9858	0.0000	4.3900
Russia	0.0119	0.0000	0.0623	144.2067	9.9944	0.0000	1.5000
South Africa	0.0854	0.0000	0.2578	38.4417	5.2196	0.0000	3.9900
Turkey	0.0653	0.0000	0.2274	304.8382	12.5042	0.0000	7.4000
Average	0.1121	0.0020	0.3205	98.0389	7.0430		

Table 22: reports the mean, median, standard deviation, kurtosis, skewness, minimum and maximum of the daily raw sky cloud cover (SKC) over the period 1996-2011. SKC is ranging from 0 to 8. 0 SKC is measured in oktas. SKC denotes the fraction of the total celestial dome covered by clouds or other obscuring phenomena.

	Mean	Median	Standard Deviation	Kurtosis	Skewness	Minimum	Maximum
Developed Countries							
Australia	4.0082	4.1250	2.4868	-1.3627	-0.1023	0.0000	8.0000
Canada	3.3838	2.8889	2.9326	-1.4586	0.2744	0.0000	8.0000
France	5.6436	6.2500	2.0506	0.3009	-1.0671	0.0000	8.0000
Germany	5.5858	6.4545	2.3317	-0.1081	-1.0107	0.0000	8.0000
Italy	4.1244	4.1250	2.5729	-1.2183	-0.0321	0.0000	8.0000
Japan	5.1803	6.5000	2.7234	-1.1274	-0.6347	0.0000	8.0000
Netherlands	5.4190	6.0909	2.3163	-0.4353	-0.8193	0.0000	8.0000
Norway	5.6342	6.2500	2.0897	-0.5610	-0.7149	0.0000	8.0000
United Kingdom	5.2411	5.7727	2.0982	-0.5093	-0.6886	0.0000	8.0000
United States	5.1188	5.6667	2.5561	-1.1213	-0.4708	0.0000	8.0000
Average	4.9339	5.4124	2.4158	-0.7601			
Emerging countries							
Brazil	5.2002	5.8889	2.3200	-0.5186	-0.7748	0.0000	8.0000
China	4.6815	5.3333	2.9508	-1.4163	-0.3271	0.0000	8.0000
Czech Republic	5.4243	6.0000	2.2320	-0.4452	-0.7616	0.0000	8.0000
India	3.2524	2.6667	2.8393	-1.4879	0.2379	0.0000	8.0000
Malaysia	6.9980	7.0000	0.1365	79.1946	-5.0344	4.0000	7.8000
Mexico	3.4817	3.5000	2.6113	-1.3012	0.1341	0.0000	8.0000
Poland	5.3976	5.8000	2.1034	-0.3629	-0.7374	0.0000	8.0000
Russia	5.7763	6.6667	2.4541	-0.4160	-0.8886	0.0000	8.0000
South Africa	3.1342	3.2000	2.1998	-1.0245	0.1076	0.0000	8.0000
Turkey	3.6944	3.7273	2.4394	-1.3057	-0.0696	0.0000	8.0000
Average	4.7041	4.9783	2.2287	7.0916			

Table 23: reports the mean, median, standard deviation, kurtosis, skewness, minimum and maximum of the daily raw sea level pressure (SLP) over the period 1996-2011. SLP is the air pressure relative to mean sea level. This is measured in hectopascals.

	Mean	Median	Standard Deviation	Kurtosis	Skewness	Minimum	Maximum
Developed Countries							
Australia	10175.32	10178.00	67.25	-0.01	-0.17	9895.88	10385.50
Canada	10163.39	10164.44	79.25	0.53	-0.17	9854.22	10449.67
France	10164.55	10169.25	91.38	0.66	-0.42	9742.50	10415.50
Germany	10165.42	10158.00	69.99	2.73	-0.19	9733.00	10418.91
Italy	10157.53	10155.94	75.78	0.40	-0.06	9829.00	10387.13
Japan	10136.14	10136.00	70.96	0.10	-0.12	9798.00	10358.50
Netherlands	10151.39	10158.95	101.00	0.53	-0.42	9666.18	10429.09
Norway	10115.50	10120.25	120.86	0.09	-0.20	9635.25	10495.50
United Kingdom	10151.02	10160.32	106.84	0.55	-0.48	9662.00	10437.55
United States	10165.74	10165.33	80.13	0.67	-0.22	9710.78	10438.00
Average	10154.60	10156.65	86.34	0.63	-0.24		
Emerging countries							
Brazil	10212.74	10181.78	116.06	1.61	1.58	10024.33	10500.00
China	10166.16	10166.67	90.30	-0.89	0.11	9938.33	10416.67
Czech Replubic	10165.93	10164.63	84.55	0.47	-0.06	9822.75	10465.25
India	10079.47	10080.67	34.40	-0.12	-0.34	9924.00	10163.67
Malaysia	10093.53	10093.20	13.83	0.19	0.19	10051.40	10142.80
Mexico	10095.82	10095.00	39.00	2.24	0.50	9986.50	10466.00
Poland	10157.94	10158.40	88.36	0.42	-0.02	9806.20	10511.40
Russia	10155.51	10148.33	106.13	0.53	0.30	9742.00	10562.00
South Africa	10188.75	10187.00	117.85	0.58	0.58	9956.50	10430.00
Turkey	10162.28	10157.00	62.53	-0.01	0.29	9962	10372
Average	10147.81	10143.27	75.30	0.50	0.31		

Table 24: reports the mean, median, standard deviation, kurtosis, skewness, minimum and maximum of the daily raw temperature (TEMP) over the period 1996-2011. TEMP is measured in Celsius for the air temperature.

	Mean	Median	Standard Deviation	Kurtosis	Skewness	Minimum	Maximum
Developed Countries							
Australia	17.1118	17.3875	4.1813	-0.8457	-0.0857	6.3625	31.0000
Canada	7.9650	7.8889	9.4521	-0.6666	-0.2797	-21.8222	26.7556
France	13.4846	13.6500	7.4256	-0.5865	-0.0403	-10.1250	35.7750
Germany	12.8401	12.9682	8.3283	-0.7776	-0.0569	-11.7273	35.0000
Italy	16.6539	16.9250	8.8879	-1.1835	-0.0704	-3.5375	35.2375
Japan	17.2404	17.4500	7.6621	-1.1366	-0.0022	0.0000	34.8500
Netherlands	12.1537	12.3955	6.8012	-0.4809	-0.0959	-9.9636	30.8182
Norway	6.9109	7.1500	9.4866	-0.6432	-0.2049	-22.6250	28.3000
United Kingdom	12.8643	12.8864	6.0025	-0.6081	-0.0178	-3.2000	30.8182
United States	12.0863	12.2278	9.3872	-0.8795	-0.1775	-14.0667	32.3556
Average	12.9311	13.0929	7.7615	-0.7808	-0.1031		
Emerging countries							
Brazil	21.0037	21.3111	3.8099	-0.4765	-0.2717	8.6333	31.0000
China	17.3891	18.3667	8.7601	-1.0943	-0.1583	-3.4000	35.5333
Czech Replubic	11.5127	11.8750	9.1872	-0.8521	-0.0900	-14.6500	34.1000
India	29.4436	29.4667	2.0101	0.1848	-0.2528	19.7333	37.8667
Malaysia	28.4727	28.5200	1.4913	-0.2921	-0.1014	23.3000	33.6200
Mexico	15.8095	15.6000	3.3783	0.0978	0.0613	4.0000	27.6500
Poland	9.9294	10.4200	9.3815	-0.7283	-0.1965	-21.4400	31.9000
Russia	6.4480	6.2667	12.6878	-0.7440	-0.2269	-30.6333	34.1667
South Africa	19.4972	19.8600	4.4545	-0.2917	-0.3508	4.0600	31.2300
Turkey	16.7529	16.5273	8.0752	-1.0582	-0.0455	-4.4818	35.2364
Average	17.6259	17.8213	6.3236	-0.5255	-0.1633		

Table 25: reports the mean, median, standard deviation, kurtosis, skewness, minimum and maximum of the daily raw visibility (VISIB) over the period 1996-2011. VISIB is the visibility for the day in miles to tenths.

	Mean	Median	Standard Deviation	Kurtosis	Skewness	Minimum	Maximum
Developed Countries							
Australia	8.2429	8.1000	1.9466	4.8989	1.1475	2.8000	24.9000
Canada	7.8670	8.7000	1.6197	2.0759	-1.6267	0.7000	9.2000
France	6.6984	6.6000	2.3169	2.7427	0.8206	0.2000	20.3000
Germany	6.2282	6.9000	1.3162	4.3470	-1.8173	0.0000	13.1000
Italy	4.9993	5.7000	2.1983	1.3257	-0.0115	0.0000	19.5000
Japan	9.1061	8.0000	5.0523	0.3862	0.9011	0.8000	30.2000
Netherlands	8.7145	7.5000	4.4193	1.6656	1.1129	0.1000	32.2000
Norway	8.2179	7.6000	4.3647	1.9199	1.4020	0.2000	32.5000
United Kingdom	8.5139	7.0000	4.9186	5.6821	2.2307	0.1000	38.7000
United States	9.0071	9.9000	1.8260	6.4832	-0.4765	0.5000	22.8000
Average	7.7595	7.6000	2.9979	3.1527			
Emerging countries							
Brazil	6.5604	6.5000	1.9732	0.0179	0.3420	1.2000	14.7000
China	10.3175	10.1000	3.2881	-0.3090	0.1889	0.3000	18.6000
Czech Republic	13.1311	12.9000	7.0215	-0.4676	0.3002	0.2000	37.3000
India	2.3014	2.2000	0.8898	31.8421	4.3665	0.9000	13.4000
Malaysia	6.5793	6.7000	1.3890	2.9061	0.1100	0.3000	15.3000
Mexico	6.5587	6.5000	1.9744	0.0162	0.3417	1.2000	14.7000
Poland	6.8964	6.7000	2.8029	3.1212	1.2013	0.1000	18.6000
Russia	20.9531	22.2000	8.3302	-0.8059	-0.5220	0.1000	33.0000
South Africa	7.4806	6.9000	2.0264	0.3591	0.7999	2.0000	14.7000
Turkey	6.1485	6.4000	0.8955	7.2182	-2.0543	0.3000	13.0000
Average	8.6927	8.7100	3.0591	4.3898			

Table 26: reports the mean, median, standard deviation, kurtosis, skewness, minimum and maximum of the daily raw wind speed rate (WIND) over the period 1996-2011. WIND is the wind speed rate, the rate of horizontal travel of air past a fixed point. It is meters per second.

	Mean	Median	Standard Deviation	Kurtosis	Skewness	Minimum	Maximum
Developed Countries							
Australia	48.2791	43.6250	21.9779	1.1836	1.0294	5.1250	174.3750
Canada	44.7828	39.3333	24.3759	1.2399	1.0936	0.0000	166.2222
France	48.3625	46.0000	19.3600	0.3640	0.6577	7.5000	149.0000
Germany	36.2542	34.0909	17.3639	0.5192	0.6664	0.0000	121.6364
Italy	19.1246	16.7500	11.7126	5.6043	1.8448	0.0000	92.0000
Japan	35.0921	33.5000	14.1756	1.8571	1.0324	5.0000	121.0000
Netherlands	54.1246	51.3182	24.8530	0.9572	0.7892	4.0909	204.0000
Norway	30.5429	27.5000	17.7042	0.9814	0.8974	0.0000	117.5000
United Kingdom	44.5014	42.3636	19.5182	0.5311	0.6781	2.7273	163.5455
United States	45.4153	41.3333	21.3474	0.9998	0.9335	1.6667	144.7778
Average	40.6480	37.5814	19.2389	1.4238			
Emerging countries							
Brazil	29.9649	28.6667	13.0477	0.2607	0.4920	0.0000	79.5556
China	31.2067	30.0000	12.7586	1.2883	0.6776	0.0000	123.3333
Czech Republic	27.4063	25.0000	13.0969	1.3781	0.9410	0.0000	107.5000
India	24.2171	24.3333	12.4805	2.7492	-0.2951	0.0000	87.3333
Malaysia	19.2021	18.6000	6.7717	0.5959	0.4434	0.0000	53.6000
Mexico	22.1179	20.0000	16.5669	132.1035	8.9077	0.0000	320.0000
Poland	39.8456	38.0000	17.5210	1.1840	0.8007	0.0000	142.0000
Russia	29.1543	26.6667	14.7899	0.5904	0.6517	0.0000	103.3333
South Africa	41.7257	39.6000	15.2680	0.7636	0.7447	2.5000	120.8000
Turkey	51.6680	48.6364	20.7569	0.1742	0.5988	2.3636	149.0000
Average	31.6509	29.9503	14.3058	14.1088			

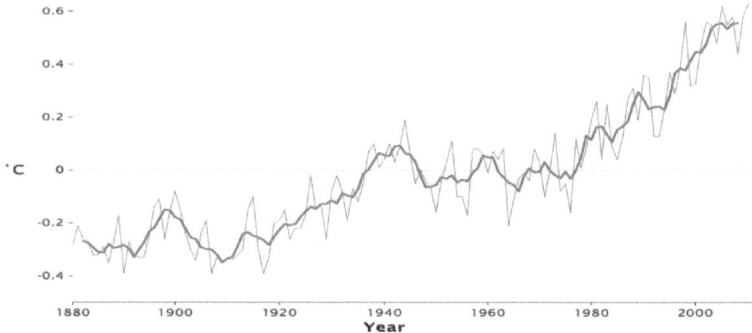

Figure 3: Global temperature anomalies (in °C). Global temperatures continue to rise at an increasing rate. The first decade of the latest millennium was the warmest decade on record. The thin line represents the annual mean, while the thick line is a five-year running mean. (source: National Aeronautics and Space Administration).